ENDORSEMENTS

Angela is raw and unfiltered in this personal narrative compelling those who are lost in the depths of despair or living in a false reality of their own creation. She bravely journeys through the layers of addiction, mental illness, and trauma to offer the possibility of freedom and redemption as a growth and healing process.

Heather Craig, MA, LPC

Angela Martin's powerful new book, *Unmasked*, moved me deeply. As I read her story—especially the account of her conversion and baptism—tears flowed freely. Again and again, I was astounded by the goodness of God, by His relentless pursuit of Angela, and by His determination to make her His and to make her whole.

Angela's story is more than a story. It is a testimony of God's deliverance, carrying the power to bring freedom to all who read it. I highly recommend *Unmasked* to everyone, but especially to those who need to be reminded once more that God loves you and is determined to save you. May Angela's story empower yours.

Steve Pixler

Author, Speaker, Senior Leader
Freedom Life Church, Mansfield, Texas

Through *Unmasked*, Angela Martin beautifully captures the process of being transformed by truth. Each chapter reveals how the masks through life's seasons can be gently removed through faith, honesty, and surrender. Her story reflects the heart of recovery. Real, raw, and redeemed by God's unrelenting love, mercy, and grace. I'm privileged to call her a friend and sister in Christ!

Daniel Brock

Combat Army Veteran, Recovery Leader

Angela is a rare example of how adversity and trauma can be transformed into grace and healing through faith. She embodies truth and healing not only in her words and actions, but just by being in her presence you can FEEL the presence of her grace. Her story will show you that regardless of circumstance, you can heal and spread that healing to others who struggle to come to terms with their past to move forward to an abundant life. She's DA BOM SHIZZLE.

Shauna Friend Worobey

Recovery Coach, MSW

Angela Martin is a dear friend and a powerful partner in the Gospel. Her testimony carries such grace and anointing. As you read *Unmasked*, I pray that the power of Angela's story will take hold of your heart and show you what God can do with those who reach out to Him for help. Angela's testimony proves God will do it!

Jeana Pixler

Author, Senior Leader and Kids Pastor
Freedom Life Church, Mansfield, Texas

Angela's story of *Unmasked* is a powerful testimony of redemption and courage. With honesty and grace, she invites readers to remove their own masks and discover the freedom found in truth and healing.

As someone personally impacted by her wisdom and faith, I can say this book beautifully reflects the heart of a woman who has allowed God to turn her pain into purpose.

Angela Rose Thorne

Author of *Unbroken*
Managing Director of Freed People

When faith meets grace, we have a decision to make. Will we allow our authentic selves to come through or maintain our performance? And so our journey begins. Not many have the courage to share their unmasking process. However, as you follow Angela Martin through her memoir, you'll find the courage to stand in front of the mirror.

It's been a personal joy to coach Angela from conception and now the birth of her incredible journey as a published author. Each chapter is littered with pearls for you to glean from. So whether you're a recovering addict or love someone who is, you'll find a refuge in these pages. A safe place to confront your fears. A safe place to remember your story. A safe place...to be *Unmasked.*

Colette Toach

Author Coach

UNMASKED

A MEMOIR OF HOPE BEYOND ABUSE, ADDICTION AND DEPRESSION

ANGELA L. MARTIN

HOPE BEYOND PRESS

For permissions or inquiries, please contact:
getrealwithangela@gmail.com

Scripture quotations are taken from the following:
Holy Bible, New King James Version® (NKJV).
Copyright © 1982 by Thomas Nelson. Used by permission. All rights reserved.

Holy Bible, New International Version® (NIV).
Copyright © 1973, 1978, 1984, 2011 by Biblica, Inc.™ Used by permission. All rights reserved worldwide.

Holy Bible, New Living Translation® (NLT).
Copyright © 1996, 2004, 2015 by Tyndale House Foundation. Used by permission of Tyndale House Publishers, Inc., Carol Stream, Illinois 60188. All rights reserved.

This is a work of nonfiction. Some names and identifying details have been changed to protect the privacy of individuals.

Editing: Melissa Chavez, *Pen of Grace Edits*
Cover Design: Steve Pixler

Photography: Lauren Marie Photography on location at Hearsay in Arlington, Texas
Interior Design: Angela L. Martin

Published by Hope Beyond Press

ISBN: 979-8-9934747-5-5
First Edition – 2025

DEDICATION

I dedicate this memoir to my children—**Ashlee, Aaron, Alysha, and Andrew.**

If there is one legacy I long to leave you, it is that of *unwavering faith* and a *warrior spirit* that never gives up. The healing I've found is for you too—every struggle faced; every tear turned to triumph, every victory shared. May you stand upon my shoulders and go farther than you could ever dream or imagine. You are my greatest joy, my deepest reason, and the living proof that God restores all things.

"*All the world's a stage, And all the men and women merely players;*
They have their exits and their entrances;
And one man in his time plays many parts."
—William Shakespeare, As You Like It (Act II, Scene VII)

CONTENTS

FOREWORD

By My Beloved

From the moment I met Angela, there was something about her I have never felt. It was like an instant connection, and I almost knew immediately I wanted her as my wife. Angela had so much determination and fire inside her that it was bigger than I ever expected.

I've had the privilege to stand beside her in great times but also the hard times when things started to be exposed. I saw her wrestle with pain and torment that I have never experienced or could believe would happen to someone.

But because of her determination, she was not willing to stay stuck in that place. Now I have seen her heal, grow, forgive, and progress into the fullness God has created her to be.

There were moments along the way when the weight of her past seemed impossible to overcome. It's amazing to see, as her husband, the transformation I have witnessed through Angela allowing God to break through all her past and set her free. It's like living with a different person now.

I'm still amazed by what God can do if you allow God to work inside of you. Seeing her today, it's hard to believe that she lived a past like she did. It's been one of the greatest honors of my life to be part of her healing story—and to be her husband through it all.

As you read *Unmasked*, you're not just holding a book. You're holding a testimony of God's relentless love and the courage it takes to live free. My prayer is that her words won't just inspire you—they'll awaken you to the truth that the same God who restored her can restore you.

With love,

David Martin

PROLOGUE

We are all invited to the stage.

Life teaches us early how to wear masks —some handed to us, others shaped by fear, pain, or the pressure to be someone we're not. These masks help us survive, perform, belong... for a time. But eventually, they suffocate us.

There comes a moment when the music fades, the lights come up, and we must decide. Will we keep hiding? Or will we dare to be seen? *Unmasked* is the story of what happens when you choose to be seen.

Woven through the metaphor of a stage play, each chapter explores a different mask I wore—and the deeper truth I discovered when I removed it. What began as a life behind masks, became a journey of being gently, yet persistently, led by God into intimacy, identity, and real connection.

For years, I didn't know who I really was beneath the roles, the trauma, or the addiction. I thought healing meant fixing myself. But I've come to learn that healing begins when we are honest with God, with ourselves, and with others. And from that place of truth, we begin to encounter the kind of love that doesn't require a mask at all.

This isn't just a memoir of pain or recovery. It's a love story. Living beyond the script and into my soul, where shame is healed, performance fades into purpose, and intimacy becomes real.

Whether you're someone who's been hiding in plain sight, performing for acceptance, or longing for deeper connection, my hope is that these pages become a mirror for your soul. That somewhere in my story, you'll find the courage to begin your own unmasking.

So welcome to the stage.

The curtains rise, the lights are dim, and the script is set in motion. Each scene reveals a mask I once wore. And with every act, a deeper truth emerges. When all the masks are gone and the performance ends, I become unashamed, unveiled, and fully alive in my true, authentic self.

Your invitation still stands.

Not just to watch, but to see yourself in the mirror of my story.

It's time to be seen.

It's time to get real.

It's time to be unmasked.

ACT 1

The Curtain Rises. The Masquerade Begins

In this first act, the curtain rises on a life shaped by masks—false identities carefully crafted to survive pain, rejection, and misunderstanding. From the "Good Girl" to the "Addict," each mask reveals the layers of struggle hidden beneath the surface. These chapters take you deep into the heart of brokenness, exposing the lies that shaped me and the battles fought in silence. It's the raw, unfiltered beginning of a story of unmasking and awakening.

CHAPTER ONE

THE MASK OF INNOCENCE

"We understand how dangerous a mask can be. We all become what we pretend to be."

—Patrick Rothfuss

The first time I felt unsafe, I was 11 years old. I was in a basement filled with liquor bottles, sitting on a worn couch with a boy who was far too old for me. A voice in me screamed, "Run," but my body wouldn't move. I was frozen. Helpless. Something inside me shifted that day. I stepped out of my childhood and into something darker. I didn't know it then, but the Mask of Innocence was already slipping.

I was born on Sunday, November 25, in Saratoga Springs, New York. My parents were kids themselves. Mom was 17 and Dad was 19 years old. To this day, my dad still reminds me of the football game that was on the day before. Michigan and Ohio State ended in a 10–10 tie. Back then, there was no overtime. Games could end in a tie.

My mom grew up in New York, and when she talks about her childhood, she calls it "good." She went to public school with her two sisters, wore dresses or skirts with knee socks, and spent hours playing outside until the streetlights came on. She told stories of simple joys, like fishing on Long Island, laying pennies on the train tracks, and waiting for the rumble of steel to crush them flat.

My grandfather, David, was raised in a Polish family in Pennsylvania. He spent some time in the United States Army, Navy, and then was going to enlist in the Air Force. That was until he met his future wife, my grandmother. She was Virginia, "Ginny," and grew up in a German family in Middle Village, Queens, New York.

I didn't get much time with my grandfather. He passed away when I was only five. The memories I do have are scattered moments from our trips to New York. Mom would pile us kids onto the Amtrak train. We'd travel through the night, lulled by the rhythmic hum of the train.

By morning, as we neared our destination, my sister and I would disappear into the large restroom with the heavy sliding door to change our clothes and brush our hair. My grandmother was waiting on the other end, full of life, full of song. She never met a stranger, and when she laughed, the whole room belonged to her.

Echoes Behind the Stage

My dad's childhood wasn't so simple. He was born in Canada after his parents left the United Kingdom, eventually crossing the Ambassador Bridge into a Detroit suburb. He grew up in the heart of the 1960s. He was the third of four kids, three boys and a favored younger sister. He spent his days playing pee-wee football and his Sundays serving as an acolyte at a Methodist church.

My grandparents were proud British. I absolutely loved showing them off to my friends. I wanted them to hear them speak with their proper British accents.

But before they were my grandparents, they were survivors.

During World War II, my grandad served in the British Navy, while my Nana fought a different kind of battle back home. She worked in the bomb factories; she pieced together weapons meant for war. When the air raid sirens screamed through the streets of London, my Nana disappeared underground and waited in the dark.

Even years later, something as simple as a song could undo her. The song "White Christmas" was unbearable to her. We learned that it carried memories of the ones who never made it home. The war may have ended, but its echoes never left her.

Back then, no one called it PTSD. No one talked about trauma. To quiet the noise of those memories, she took sedatives for her nerves. She was simply expected to move on. And she did, the best way she knew how.

Tiptoeing Through Childhood

My parents moved to Michigan when I was very young. I have fond memories of playing in our suburban neighborhood, where I had friends on every block. My sisters and I would often create dance routines to our favorite songs and practice until it was time to perform for our extended family.

Amidst the laughter, an undercurrent lingered in our home, dictated by my father's ever-shifting moods. He drank daily. My father worked tirelessly in an auto factory to provide for our family. When it came to emotional presence, he was absent. I understand now that you can't give away what you don't possess. My sister and I would come home from elementary school, carefully tiptoeing into the house and nervously ask my mom, "Is Dad mad?"

I wanted my dad to see me. I wanted him to be proud of me. So, I tried to become the kind of daughter he'd want to brag about. At school, I poured myself into every assignment, earning straight A's. I studied his interests and made them my own.

I chased his attention through music, sports, and anything that made me feel closer to him. I laced up skates for girls' ice hockey, sat beside him watching NASCAR, and played his favorite records over and over. I even picked up a guitar, trying to learn the language of music that moved him so deeply.

When I was 11, my dad made me cassette tapes of my favorite band, *Led Zeppelin I and II*, a gift that felt like a special connection to his world. Mom wasn't thrilled about some of the lyrics, so he recorded bits of the radio over those parts.

I didn't know it then, but I was already wearing my first mask, the Good Girl Mask. If I could just become the daughter he was proud of, maybe he'd see me. Maybe he'd love me the way I needed him to.

When Heaven Called

My mom had this strong faith that I didn't fully understand. It all started when she was a teenager. A friend's mom shared the Gospel with her in a way she had never heard before, and it changed her life. Over the years, that faith grew stronger, and she made sure we children went to church every Sunday. She'd send us on the bus to the local Baptist church, hoping it would plant the seed of faith in us.

After a while, Mom decided to start attending a Church of God denomination church. She took all four of us siblings with her. Dad didn't go, so our home always felt divided.

One summer, my sister and I went to the church camp. That's where I first really felt God's presence. I remember standing there, surrounded by kids I barely knew, when the worship music started. I felt this overwhelming presence fill the room, like God Himself had walked in.

They invited people to the front to pray, and something inside tugged at my heart. I didn't know exactly what was happening, but I didn't want that feeling to pass, so I invited Jesus into my heart. Everything felt so peaceful, like a warm blanket of love surrounding me. This moment wasn't just a Sunday school lesson. It was real. I was marked.

God was calling me, I knew it was significant, even if I didn't fully understand it.

... and Darkness Answered

Not long after that camp experience, something else happened that I wasn't prepared for. It was no coincidence that at the very moment

I opened the door to faith, darkness came knocking. Music quickly became a world I disappeared into. It became both an escape and a portal into something darker.

Alone in my room, I'd sink into a trance while listening to The Doors. I read *No One Here Gets Out Alive* by Jerry Hopkins and Danny Sugerman and felt something dark stirring inside me. It almost felt like worship. I didn't know it at the time, but I was opening myself to an undercurrent of despair, letting it seep deep into my spirit.

I withdrew to my room more and more, wanting to be alone. I picked up a pen and began to write poetry. It became a safe place to pour out my swirling emotions, tinged with a sense of longing I couldn't quite explain. The deeper I leaned into the dark presence, the more I wrote poetry laced with the same haunted energy I was feeling.

I've been trying to find words for it ever since, but all I can say is that there was darkness in that room. A presence was there offering me an invitation to another realm.

The War for My Innocence

I wasn't just a confused 11-year-old. That moment wasn't random. I was in the middle of a spiritual battle I didn't even know how to fight. Unfortunately, my young will gave way to the tantalizing lure of the world, an unknown force that seemed to empower me.

It wasn't a coincidence that the first time I drank alcohol, got drunk, and had my first experience with a teenage boy all happened right after I encountered God. Something shifted, and I began feeling driven to extremes. I like to describe it as the point when I started coloring outside the lines. While most people stuck to the usual boundaries, I began stepping beyond them, making choices that didn't fit the norm.

One school night when I was 11, I was at a friend's house, hanging out in his basement. There was a full liquor bar. I remember drinking the liquor and eventually being coerced into a bed where I was touched inappropriately. Everything inside of me wanted to run, but somewhere in that moment I was frozen and felt helpless.

The lack of protection became a silent invitation, an open door I didn't know how to close. I found myself in places where boundaries didn't exist, and in the spaces between childhood and something far too grown. It was often at the houses of girlfriends, where older brothers and their friends lurked just beyond the edges of supervision.

By 12, I had learned how to disappear. The moment my dad left for his second-shift job and my mom retreated to her room for the night, I was slipping through the back door. I would pedal into the darkness on my bike from safety and deeper into a world I wasn't ready for.

Reflection

At some point, we all learn that not everyone—and not everything—can
be trusted. The moment innocence breaks
is the moment we start hiding.

The Lie Behind the Mask

"If I act good enough, I can keep bad things from happening."

The Truth

True safety isn't found in pretending—it's found in the presence of the
One who sees behind every mask.

Psalm 139:1 (NKJV)
O Lord, You have searched me and known me.

CHAPTER TWO

THE GOOD GIRL'S SCRIPT

"The whole world is a masquerade; disguises are an art."
—Lucian of Samosata

There were cracks in the surface, even during those carefree childhood days. Beneath the laughter and carefully choreographed dance routines, I often felt a restlessness that I now recognize as signs of a dysfunctional family system.

A dysfunctional family is one where healthy boundaries are blurred, roles are confused, and pain often gets passed down instead of healing. In these homes, love is conditional; communication is strained or unsafe, and unspoken rules like "don't feel, don't speak, and don't trust" shape how everyone survives.

Instead of being a place of safety and connection, the family becomes a stage where denial, blame, and silence are the main characters. In my family, my father was a "functioning alcoholic," while my mother fit the profile of a classic "codependent." At 12-Step meetings, I introduce myself as an adult child of family dysfunction, because that's where the roots of my story begin.

The chaos at home left its mark. My father's unpredictable moods and daily drinking shaped how I learned to navigate the world with extreme caution and fear. Anxiety was my constant companion, though I didn't have the words to describe it then.

My hobbies became more than just pastimes; they were distractions, a way to lose myself in something that didn't require me to confront the fear and insecurity brewing inside.

That anxiety was a silent teacher, training me to expect disappointment and brace for impact, even in moments of peace. I was learning how to live in survival mode, anticipating the next storm. It was exhausting. I did my best to keep it together. But the sadness was there, hidden behind my smile. Beneath it all, fear gnawed at me. It was always there. Like a silent scream inside my chest.

My obsessive nail-biting and the compulsion to pull out my eyelashes were early signals that something inside me was unraveling. I chewed my nails down to the skin and yanked out my eyelashes one by one. I'll never forget the night my father noticed. We were at the dinner table when his eyes locked onto my bare eyelids. In front of everyone, he asked, "What is wrong with you?"

I had no answer. Just the familiar sting of shame crawling up my throat. I didn't understand what was happening inside me. I only knew that whatever it was, it was something to be ashamed of. And so, I buried it deeper.

Silent Inheritance

I grew up watching my parents live behind their masks; my father's were soaked in alcohol, numbing the wounds of a childhood he seldom talked about, but I knew existed. My mother's mask was staying busy, taking care of my three younger siblings, and doing whatever she could to keep my father happy.

Trauma raised trauma in our home, passed down like an heirloom no one wanted but no one knew how to let go of. Generational trauma was the open door, one that shaped us while teaching us to deny what hurt. We learned to mask our pain before we even had the words to name it, to absorb the chaos without question.

Choreographed Smiles - Learning to Play the Part

The Good Girl Mask was the first mask I ever wore. Before I even understood what a mask was, I had already learned to put one on. Somewhere deep inside, I believed that if I was obedient and pleasing to others, I would be safe and maybe even loved. My inner dialogue whispered, "If I'm good enough, I'll be loved."

That quiet vow shaped everything. I chased straight A's as my father incentivized me with the promise of earning ten dollars for each one. The mask fit so well I didn't realize it had started to define me.

As I grew older, the mask hardened into perfectionism. I did everything I could to excel in school and sports, particularly in softball and girls' ice hockey, activities I hoped would capture my father's attention. I didn't realize it then, but I had exchanged one performance for another. If I could be the best, the brightest, the most talented, then maybe I would be noticed.

But underneath all the striving was rejection. No matter how hard I worked, I couldn't make my dad put the bottle down. I couldn't make my mom sit still. I couldn't fix what was broken in my home or inside of me with perfect grades or game-winning goals. So, I kept performing, mastering the script, becoming whoever I needed to be in each room. I wore each mask, carefully switching them out as the spotlight shifted.

To my teachers, coaches, and friends, I was the hardworking, determined achiever. But inside, I was a scared, confused child desperately seeking love and acceptance. Praise became my drug of choice. It dulled the ache inside, the nagging feeling that I wasn't truly loved, but only approved of when I performed. But even the best performances can't protect a fragile heart forever.

The breaking point came when my goodness was no longer enough to shield me from pain. Whether it was betrayal from friends or being taken advantage of in my vulnerability, I began to suffocate under the very mask I thought would protect me.

I wasn't okay. But I didn't dare show it.

Admitting the truth felt like failure. Like I had let everyone down, including God. But what surfaced in the place of unraveling was both heartbreaking and liberating. I was hurt, and it wasn't my fault! The abuse, the manipulation, the deep ache of rejection, none of it happened because I wasn't good enough. It was because broken people inflict their brokenness on others. Taking off this mask would take years, but it began here, with the shattering of my illusion that being good could save me.

A Truth to Behold

In one way or another, we're all forced to perform. We build masks to make others feel comfortable, make us feel safe, or help us survive. How about you? Maybe you learned early how to perform or how to become what others expected, even when it cost you pieces of yourself. We mold ourselves into the image others expect, often at the expense of the image God intended.

Perhaps, like me, you longed to be seen, to be chosen, to be enough. Maybe your mask was perfection, or rebellion, or silence. Maybe it was the careful construction of a life that looked fine on the outside but felt hollow within.

Reflection

I invite you to sit with your own reflection. Not to shame yourself,
but to be curious and compassionate.
What if the parts you've spent years trying to cover, are the very places
God wants to breathe life?
Who taught you that goodness equals worthiness—and what did it cost
your heart?

The Lie Behind the Mask

"If I perform instead of allowing myself to be real and imperfect,
then I'll be accepted."

The Truth

You are already loved.

Jeremiah 31:3 (NKJV)
The Lord has appeared of old to me, saying:
"Yes, I have loved you with an everlasting love;
Therefore with lovingkindness I have drawn you."

CHAPTER THREE

CAST AS THE SCAPEGOAT

"Shame is the most powerful, master emotion. It's the fear that we're not good enough."
—Brené Brown

In dysfunctional families, there's often one person who gets blamed for everything that's wrong—the scapegoat. They carry the weight no one else wants to face: the shame, the chaos, and the unspoken pain. It's a pattern as old as Scripture. In Leviticus, the scapegoat was sent into the wilderness, symbolically bearing the sins of the people. In my family, that person was me.

I first heard the term at Al-Anon meetings, which offer support for families of Alcoholics Anonymous (AA) members. My mom began attending meetings, looking for peace in the storm of my dad's drinking. Not long after, we kids started joining her. We attended Alateen (a support group for teens with family members struggling with alcoholism) in another room.

I remember sitting in a circle of strangers, listening to words like powerless and boundaries, but all I really felt was confused. What no one said out loud was what I felt. Something was wrong, and somehow, it was landing on me. The Scapegoat Mask isn't just about being blamed. It's about being miscast in your own story.

As I've been writing this memoir, old, buried wounds have started rising to the surface. I set out to write a legacy book, trace generational patterns, and confront more truth about how the family systems we grow up in shape us in hopes of providing answers and strategies to move towards wholeness.

I earned a Bachelor of Arts in Family Life Education, which gave me language and insight. But nothing has taught me quite like life and recovery. That has finally helped me begin to answer the "why" I've wrestled with for years. Lately, that "why" has been leading me back further than I expected, back into generational layers I didn't know were there.

When Favor Feels Like Blame

As I mentioned in the first chapter, my father was the third son, born before the fourth child, the family's favored youngest daughter. I was the first grandchild on that side of the family, and my Nana's favoritism was obvious—so blatant, in fact, that it was clear to my siblings as well.

But now I'm asking, did the favor Nana have for me echo the favor she once had for her daughter, my aunt? And did that favor put me in an awkward position within my own family, especially with my father? I'm starting to see that the scapegoat role isn't always about being rejected. Sometimes, being the one who sees clearly is the problem.

The spirit of jealousy was no stranger to our bloodline; it had been passed through the generations. I was favored from birth, while my little sister, born just nine days before my first birthday, was not. Jealousy is a murderous spirit, as old as the biblical story of Cain and Abel, and it had taken root in our family long before I was born. It was in our blood, and it wasn't leaving anytime soon.

When you carry discernment, you become a mirror. And mirrors make people uncomfortable when they're not ready to face what's being reflected. The harder I tried to be good, the more it seemed like I was the problem. And not long after, the Mask of Blame sealed itself to my face.

By then, I had already started slipping through the cracks. I became the one who "acted out," but really, I was just living out the role I had been handed. The one who carried the family's unspoken pain so no one else had to.

I learned that if I couldn't be the good one, I might as well be the wild one. So, I kept sneaking out of the house. I knew which floorboards creaked, avoiding them like land mines. I mastered how to close the back door without it making a sound. I didn't know it yet, but I was writing scenes into my story that would scar me for years to come.

The Scene I Never Rehearsed

There was one night that changed everything. I pedaled to my "boyfriend's" house, a boy a few years older than me, already growing a beard. He lived with his mom, a single parent who wasn't home. We sat on the couch watching *The Song Remains the Same*, and he handed me a joint like it was no big deal.

I took a hit and coughed a little, but I was already used to cigarettes by then. I inhaled deeply, like it was nothing new. What happened next, I've tried to forget a thousand times. Everything felt distorted, like the room was bending around me, but I stayed quiet. Then, somewhere between the blur and the silence, it happened. He raped me. I went numb.

I wanted to pretend it didn't happen and ignore the blood I saw when I went to the restroom. I wanted to erase it, forget it, bury it. And that's exactly what I did. I told myself I was to blame. That it was my fault for sneaking out. My fault for being high. I wore that shame like skin. But writing this book has forced me to tell the truth: I was a child. I was 12. I was raped.

That night, I fastened the Scapegoat Mask. It became a false identity, one that told me his sin was mine to carry. I bore the burden of guilt that didn't belong to me. As a child, I didn't have the language or the capacity to process what happened.

So, I buried it—deep in my soul. I accepted abuse and rejection as my portion because something inside me believed I had brought it on myself. That lie shaped how I saw myself. It shaped how I let others treat me from that point forward.

No Longer Playing the Part

Breaking free from the emotional landfill of scapegoating hasn't come easy. It's taken years to untangle what I carried from what was never mine in the first place. The shame and blame I took on throughout life were never mine to hold. Jesus already carried that weight for me. I just didn't know how to lay it down.

I've had to reclaim my identity and believe that I was never a problem to be fixed. I was a voice that needed to be heard. I don't owe anyone a performance. Jesus didn't perform for people's sake. On the contrary, He was hated and crucified for exposing what others wanted to keep hidden. He has always been the way to freedom and is now my strength to speak out.

A Truth to Behold

Here's the truth I need you to hear if you've ever walked in my shoes:

I didn't deserve what happened to me.

And neither did you.

Your silence was survival, not consent.

Your trauma was not your fault.

You were never meant to carry someone else's guilt.

We are not responsible for repenting for someone else's sin.

Reflection

What moments have you carried shame that never belonged to you? Ask God to reveal where you've taken ownership of pain that wasn't yours to bear—and to replace it with His truth about who you are.

The Lie Behind the Mask

"I am unworthy because of what was done to me; I am defined by others' rejection and shame."

The Truth

You are chosen and beloved, not cast out.

Romans 8:33-34; 38-39 (NKJV)

33 Who dares accuse us whom God has chosen for his own? No one—for God himself has given us right standing with himself. 34 Who then will condemn us? No one—for Christ Jesus died for us and was raised to life for us, and he is sitting in the place of honor at God's right hand, pleading for us.

38 And I am convinced that nothing can ever separate us from God's love. Neither death nor life, neither angels nor demons, neither our fears for today nor our worries about tomorrow—not even the powers of hell can separate us from God's love. 39 No power in the sky above or in the earth below—indeed, nothing in all creation will ever be able to separate us from the love of God that is revealed in Christ Jesus our Lord.

CHAPTER FOUR

THE PEOPLE-PLEASER'S MASK

"**I**f you live for their approval, you'll die by their rejection."

—Unknown

I want to begin this next section by expressing my deep love, respect, and admiration for my parents. They, like all of us, faced their own struggles and came from families with their own challenges. No family is perfect; each of us carries some degree of dysfunction.

In recovery, I've learned to describe myself as "an adult child of family dysfunction who struggles with addiction, mental illness, and shame." Some of the typical characteristics that shaped my upbringing included:

- Parents who struggled with mental illness or substance abuse.
- Abusive or emotionally immature behavior from parents.
- Persistent conflicts and unresolved issues.
- Emotional extremes—either intense outbursts or complete emotional suppression.

The best way to sum it up? Don't feel, don't talk, don't trust.

Scaling the Tightrope

Growing up as the oldest of four in a family with an alcoholic father and a codependent mother, felt like walking a tightrope every day. Without realizing it, I slipped on the People-Pleaser Mask. If I could keep everyone happy, if I could become who they needed me to be, then maybe I wouldn't feel so invisible. And maybe I could make the chaos go away.

I bore the weight of responsibility, often stepping into a caregiver role for my younger siblings while striving to maintain peace at home. The experience left its mark on me in ways I wouldn't understand until much later.

I thought my survival depended on doing whatever was necessary to keep the household functioning. But what I didn't realize was that the more I adapted, the more I buried my own needs and identity. Survival came at the cost of my sense of self, and it would take years to unearth who I truly was beneath the roles I had been forced to play. Eventually, this dynamic shifted, and my sister took on the caregiver role while I continued to embody the classic scapegoat.

Moments of laughter and joy existed, but they were often over-shadowed by the tension stemming from my father's drinking and my mother's relentless need to keep things under control. My father even came up with a song that's still stuck in our heads to this day. We'd all sing along, chanting, "Under control," and we'd echo back, "Under control," until he'd finish with, "Your mother has it under control."

It became one of those silly family songs we couldn't help but re-member. Beneath the surface of that catchy tune, however, was a text-book codependent trait, a fear that everything might fall apart. The reas-surance was less about control and more about managing our collective anxiety.

I learned to navigate the chaos, tiptoeing around emotional land-mines and developing a keen sense of what to say—or not say—to avoid triggering conflict. It felt as if I were always on guard, acting out scapegoat behaviors while suppressing my own feelings. This juggling act shaped my childhood, leaving me confused about what a "normal" fam-ily truly looked like. The confusion didn't end there. I often questioned myself: "Was it me? Was I the problem?"

When you grow up in dysfunction, you begin to internalize the chaos. You believe that if you were just better, quieter, or more helpful, everything would improve. It's a heavy burden for a child to bear, and it fosters a deep sense of inadequacy.

I hardly ever invited friends over or invited them to spend the night. The thought of them seeing my home life was overwhelming, and I was paralyzed by the fear of what they might think. That's what the People-Pleaser Mask did. It convinced me that if I could just appear normal to the outside world, maybe I could become normal.

I could control how others saw me, even if I couldn't control what happened at home. I said yes when I wanted to say no. Smiled when I felt dead inside. Made myself small to avoid conflict. I spent as much time away as I could, enjoying the moments free of worry and fear.

Yet, when it was time to return home, a tight knot of anxiety would erupt in my stomach. It was supposed to be a place of safety, but instead, it felt like a war zone. I often wished I could stay out just a little longer, searching for excuses to avoid coming back, or simply retreating to my room to "stay out of the way".

Highs, Lies, and Hidden Cries

A troubling pattern of drug and alcohol abuse began to emerge during my preteens. At the age of only 11, I came home drunk for the first time on a school night. By the time I turned 12, I had started smoking marijuana.

I picked up cigarettes earlier than that, swiping them from my dad's soft pack. I became an expert at folding the foil back just right to hide any evidence of my theft. These behaviors weren't just acts of rebellion—they were cries for help. I was desperate for relief, searching for something, anything, that could dull the pain and confusion I felt every day. At that age, I didn't have the words to articulate my struggles, so I turned to substances to speak for me.

There was a battle for my destiny long before I ever understood it. God had marked me, set me apart for His purposes, and the enemy was already working overtime to take me out. I thought I was just a teenager pushing the limits, but I was already under the weight of something much heavier.

I had another unforgettable experience at church that still lingers in my memory. By this time, I was in full-blown rebellion, and I didn't even want to be there. That day, a guest minister from Peniel Ministries came to speak. She was a middle-aged woman, sharp and full of authority. Midway through the service, she locked eyes with me from across the room and started walking in my direction. I felt my stomach drop.

When she got to me, she didn't hesitate. With a stern voice, she said, "If you don't stop doing drugs, you're going to end up on a road of destruction far away from God!"

I froze.

How did she know? I hadn't told a soul about what I was into. My mom sat there beside me hearing every word. Still, I didn't stop. I wasn't ready to listen. If anything, the darkness around me seemed to tighten its grip. The thrill of the drugs, the rush of attention, and the high of rebellion still had me by the throat.

By 13, my drinking and marijuana use had escalated rapidly. Somehow, the local party store had no problem selling me bottles of liquor—Jim Beam, Jack Daniels—you name it. It still blows my mind that I could walk in, hand over cash, and walk out with booze like it was nothing.

The owner of the store was actually one of my *Detroit Free Press* paper route customers. Maybe that's why he didn't ask questions. Or maybe he just didn't care. Either way, I took full advantage of it.

Eager to impress, I'd stuff the bottles in my bag and head straight to my boyfriend's house. There was a rush to it. The adrenaline of sneaking around, the thrill of knowing I could get caught. Sharing the liquor with my boyfriends made me feel cool and desirable. It gave me a sense of power, like I had something they wanted. But really, it was fuel for the People-Pleaser Mask.

I was already caught in the performance of trying to be liked so I could feel loved. The mask whispered lies like: "If I'm likable, I'll be loved. If I fit in, I'll belong."

Hope Came, Then It Left

My father, caught in his own battle with alcohol, made the decision to check himself into Henry Ford Maple Grove Center, an addiction treatment center. Part of his recovery involved family sessions, which meant we were all pulled into the process.

During one of those meetings, the counselors turned their attention to me. They saw something in my behavior and recommended that my mom and dad enroll me in the juvenile program. They hoped it would get me back on track and stop me from heading down the same destructive path.

I didn't want to be away from home, away from my friends, but for the first time, I found a place where I felt like I belonged. The adults there actually listened. They weren't trying to manipulate me or use me. They just cared. I felt the discomfort of the Mask of Rejection I was wearing and tried to pull it away. For a moment, it felt like my mask started to crack. Maybe I didn't have to keep pretending.

For the first time in my life, I saw my dad sober. It felt like a glimpse into a world I had never known, one where hope wasn't just something other families had. Recovery gave us a new bond, something just ours, something real. But it didn't last.

My dad went back to drinking, and the disappointment hit me like a brick to the chest. The betrayal burned, and I let my anger loose. We fought, our words sharp and our emotions raw, until he finally told me to leave. So, I did.

I ran straight to my sponsor's house, where she took me in without hesitation. I told my mom where I was so she wouldn't worry, but I made sure she didn't tell my dad. I wanted him to feel my absence. I wanted him to wonder if I was ok. A week passed before I went home. The door was open, but something between us had closed.

The Scapegoat Returns

Despite the intervention, my life spiraled again. I was going to Alcoholics Anonymous and Narcotics Anonymous meetings. I sat in a circle of broken stories, trying to work my teenage recovery program. That's where I met him. He was 22. He offered attention that felt like affection.

At first, it felt like safety. But it was manipulation. It was something far more dangerous than I was capable of understanding. I started sneaking out again. Same pattern, different face. I'd meet him around the corner in the middle of the night and slip back in before the sun came up, pretending like everything was normal.

I was a young girl trying to fill an aching void with anything that looked like love.

But here I am again, tempted to minimize what happened. To make it sound like teenage rebellion, like I knew what I was doing. I never lied about my age. I wasn't high. I was 14. He was 22. He raped me repeatedly. And I believed it was my fault.

I had internalized the label, "rebellious child," and with twisted pride, I was proud to have the scapegoat role in our family. But it also came with bearing the burdens of others and the belief that I was the cause of my pain, the architect of my own violations.

Recalling those nights, how I kept lying there, twists my stomach with anger for little Angela. But I'm learning to shout the truth without flinching: I was not to blame. I was a child.

He didn't love me. He moved on to other girls in recovery. Even to my own sponsor. What I thought was connection was just convenience. I wasn't special. I was available. And the meetings that were supposed to help me heal were ripe with broken people looking to fill voids in each other.

Hope in a New Place

That summer, our family packed up and headed to upstate New York to visit my aunt, uncle, and three cousins. It was supposed to be a short getaway. A break from the chaos back home. But as the days passed, a thought began to take root: *What if I didn't go back? What if I could leave behind the bad decisions and the trail of mistakes that seemed to follow me everywhere?*

One evening, the thoughts materialized into words and slipped out. "What if I just stayed here? Started over?" I painted a picture of a new version of me—one who made better choices, who didn't give in to temptation. To my surprise, my parents agreed. The plan was set: I would stay in New York for my sophomore year while they worked toward their dream of leaving Dearborn Heights behind for a quieter life in the country.

Sophomore year felt like a blank slate. Like a chance to rewrite my story. I stayed sober, showed up to counseling, and even started guitar lessons, convincing myself that this fresh start could erase the wreckage of my past.

My older cousin set the standard. He was the star pitcher, in the National Honor Society; the kind of guy teachers and principals looked up to. And by association, they respected me too. I liked being seen as someone worth something.

My uncle made sure I never missed a concert, buying tickets to every hair band that came through town—Bon Jovi, Whitesnake, Aerosmith, Def Leppard. I screamed every lyric like scripture. Whether it was the roar of an arena or a crowded outdoor amphitheater, I lived for the rush of rock and roll. It wasn't just music—it was my religion.

Church was nonnegotiable. I had two options: attend my grandmother's forty-five-minute Catholic service or go with my aunt and uncle to their marathon "Soul Saving Station." The choice was easy. I went with Grandma, following her lead—stand, sit, kneel—pretending I knew what it all meant.

I kept my distance from the stoner crowd, determined to stay on the straight and narrow. Instead, I found a friend. A country girl with a big heart and a simple kind of joy. Afternoons at her house turned into weekends, and soon her older brother's circle of friends became mine. That's when one of them started paying me attention, and I was hooked.

The Pull of the Past

It started small. Keg beer at a bonfire. A joint passed around. I told myself it was harmless, but deep down I knew better. The pull of the past was stronger than my fragile resolve. Before long, I slipped back into old habits.

Soon, I was right back where I swore I'd never be. The faces were different, but the story was the same. Off-campus lunches turned into sneaking across the street to the field where the stoners gathered. I'd drift back to math class, reeking of weed. Some days, my teacher would look at me with concern and ask if I was okay.

I wasn't. But I nodded anyway.

My boyfriend—a high school dropout—and I were inseparable. My aunt and uncle saw trouble coming and, along with my parents, feared history would repeat itself. They tightened the rules, but I broke them, sneaking out whenever I could to be with him.

Then came the news: my parents had found their dream property. Six acres of wooded land and they were taking me with them that summer. No debate, no choice.

Leaving him, leaving my friends, felt like my world was being torn away. But the letters my dad sent softened the blow. In them, he wrote about the home he was preparing for me. He described how peaceful it was, how he couldn't wait for me to see it. It felt like he was building more than a house; he was creating a place where I could finally belong.

Reflection

Whose approval have you chased at the expense of your soul?

The Lie Behind the Mask

"I must fix, control, or please others to be accepted."

The Truth

God's delight in you is not performance-based.
You are loved because you are His.

Galatians 1:10 (NIV)
"Am I now trying to win the approval of human beings, or of God? If I were still trying to please people, I would not be a servant of Christ."

Chapter Five

SHATTERED IDENTITY

"We wear the mask that grins and lies,

it hides our cheeks and shades our eyes."

—Paul Laurence Dunbar

In the same way I was looking for a new start, my parents too were ready to start anew and leave the bustle of suburban Detroit behind. The house we were living in, the one my father grew up in, felt too small. It was crowded. Not just with us, but with the ghosts of his childhood.

When he came to bring me home that summer, the move to the country felt like stepping into another world.

My sister and I would stand at the edge of our property, laughing as we'd say, "Look, another car!" It was a rare sight on our long, dusty road, making every passing vehicle feel like an event.

The air was thick with the scent of farmland, and the rhythms of life were quieter, more predictable. But for my sister and me, fresh from the city, we stood out like neon signs. Our stylish clothes and big-city confidence made us instant curiosities.

Some students joked that we were undercover NARC officers, too polished to belong among the flannel shirts and worn-out jeans. The guys welcomed us right away, but earning the trust of the girls took more time.

Eventually, I found my place. Life in this small town started to feel good. I made a few close girlfriends but had just as many guy friends. By fall, my sister and I were both elected to the homecoming court—her as a sophomore, me as a junior. On game night, we rode through the stadium in borrowed convertible Corvettes, then stepped onto the field, escorted by our father and grandfather. It was one of those moments that made me feel like I truly belonged.

Maybe this new life was working out after all.

Part of what made me feel admired was the car I drove, my dad's former white 1986 Monte Carlo SS. That car was a statement. The guys at school begged me to take it for a spin, convincing me to burn out the tires in the parking lot just to hear them screech. I loved the attention, the feeling of being the cool girl with the fast car.

By the end of junior year, I pushed my luck even further. I had the audacity to run for senior class president against the reigning three-year officer, who would later graduate as valedictorian. I stood before my classmates, delivering my speech without notecards, realizing for the first time that I had a natural gift for speaking. To my surprise, I won!

That confidence carried me forward, but so did the thrill of risk-taking. At a party, I met a boy who had dropped out of high school a year ahead of me. We connected instantly, and before long, we were inseparable. While I held the title of future senior class president, I also had the nerve to bring my high school dropout boyfriend as my date to the junior dance.

My new boyfriend, Craig, lived with his father and younger siblings, a single dad doing his best to hold things together. Their house sat right in the heart of our tiny town, population 2,000, where the only traffic control was a single blinking light. But that house was anything but quiet. It was the infamous "party house," a place where older guys gathered to drink, smoke, and jam out in a garage-turned-rock-stage.

The air was thick with cigarette smoke, the scent of marijuana lingered in every corner, and beer flowed as freely as the music. Even though I was still a teenager living at home, the party never really ended, it just paused until the next night.

The Party Girl Mask I wore was crafted from a mixture of rebellion and reckless fun. I was the girl who showed up with a mischievous grin and a drink in hand, ready to push boundaries and test limits. On the surface, it looked like freedom, like I had it all under control.

In everyday situations, this mask slipped on as easily as my jeans. I was always the one pushing for the next high, the next risk. Whether it was sneaking out after curfew or turning every casual hangout into something wilder, I wore that mask proudly. It was my shield and my way of avoiding the gnawing emptiness I felt inside.

The summer before my senior year of high school marked the darkest chapter of my life. It was August 29th and what started as a carefree night spiraled into a nightmare I could never wake from.

After spending the entire day drinking vodka at the small-town community event, my friend Julie and I decided, around 11:00 p.m., to join a scavenger hunt in a nearby town. Even though I knew I had been drinking, I made the reckless decision to drive my boyfriend's truck. I vaguely remembered another friend asking, "You okay to drive?" God—why didn't I say no? All I can think is how desperately I wished someone had stopped me.

The Crash That Shattered More Than Metal

I foolishly believed taking a backroad would make it safer, but that one choice became the turning point of everything. I remember the faint sense of the road beneath the tires, the truck bouncing unsteadily along the two-lane highway, the speed limit set at 55 mph. The Ford Ranger, an extended cab, wasn't built for that kind of rough, uneven pavement.

I was driving in a blackout, my blood alcohol level later determined to be a dangerously high .18 to .2. My vision was blurry, my thoughts muddled and lost in a haze of alcohol. The blackout took away my ability to remember what was happening and how I got to that point in the road.

The road stretched endlessly between fields of farmland, a long path with nothing to guide me. I had no idea how long I'd been driving, but we hadn't made it more than a couple of miles down the road. I don't recall the truck swerving, but I lost control.

I woke up to the sound of silence. The truck in the ditch on the opposite side of the road right side up. My seatbelt held me in place, but the force of the crash had left me disoriented and gasping for air. The vehicle had rolled multiple times. My heart raced in panic as I slowly began to comprehend what had happened.

I turned my head to the right, expecting to see Julie next to me, but she wasn't there! The seat beside me was empty, and the dread that filled me was instant. Panic surged through me as I stumbled out, screaming her name into the darkness. After what felt like an eternity, I found her lying face down in a ditch. My knees gave way as I realized the gravity of the situation.

Barefoot and desperate, I ran to the nearest house, pounding on the door. No one answered. I turned and ran down the road, shards of glass cutting into my feet with every step. The pain was nothing compared to the terror consuming me.

Finally, headlights appeared in the distance, and in a panic, I waved my arms frantically, desperate for help. To my shock, it was my sister's boyfriend who pulled over. I was shaking, barely able to speak, but I tried to direct him toward my friend in the ditch. As he got closer and saw Julie, I could see the shock hit him. He stopped in his tracks, and for a moment, it felt like time froze. I could only watch as he rushed toward her, to assess what I already feared.

I have no memory of the ambulance ride to the hospital. When I came to, a nurse was scrubbing shards of glass from my feet. That's when I learned that Julie's injuries were severe. She was airlifted to a specialized facility, and soon after, the devastating news arrived: she had a spinal cord injury.

Julie stayed in the hospital from August until after Thanksgiving. I still remember the first time I went to visit her. Walking down that long, sterile hallway, my heart pounding so hard I thought it might crack open. I braced myself for what I'd see, but nothing could prepare me for her family's eyes. Her parents. Her siblings. The weight of their grief was suffocating. I wanted it to just be a nightmare that we could all wake up from.

But it was real.

I stood there, frozen, staring at Julie in the bed. I approached her and choked out the words, "I'm so sorry." She looked in my eyes, not with anger, not with blame, but with something I didn't deserve. "It's okay," she said softly. "This wasn't your fault."

Her kindness broke me. Instead of chastising me, she comforted me.

The doctors held on to hope. They planned a spinal cord surgery—the same one that had restored Gloria Estefan's ability to walk. I clung to that like a lifeline. Maybe she'd get her miracle too. But she didn't.

Then came the night at my mom's church in Ohio. A minister was in town, known to operate in the spiritual gifts of healing and miracles. I invited her, desperate to make this right. We went down to the front when the altar call came. I fell to my knees weeping, "God, please! Please!! Do for Julie what You did for others in the Bible!"

Nothing happened.

Lessons Written in Pain

At my lawyer's recommendation and in a desperate attempt to prove I was taking responsibility; I spent the first month of my senior year in a substance abuse treatment center. My dad promised me it was just an evaluation. "They're not going to keep you," he assured me. "We just have to go through the process." I believed him. But when the facility recommended that I be admitted for treatment, everything inside me snapped.

I remember that locked room closing in around me. Panic turned to rage. I pounded my fists against the wall, screaming at my dad, "You lied to me! You said you weren't going to leave me here!" I kept yelling, desperate for him to change his mind. But he didn't.

When the fight drained out of me and I finally accepted my fate, all I wanted was one last cigarette. The facility had a strict no-smoking policy for anyone under 18, but I begged my dad to let me step outside. The counselors warned him, "If you take her out there, she'll run." But he trusted me. We walked out to the parking garage. I lit my cigarette, inhaling like it was the last bit of freedom I'd ever breathe.

The aftermath was a blur of courtrooms and consequences. Initially charged with a felony, felonious driving, the charges were later reduced to two misdemeanors, reckless driving and operating under the influence of liquor. No legal judgment could compare to the guilt I carried. I wasn't in prison, but I was serving a life sentence in my own mind.

Returning to school for my senior year felt like stepping into a war zone. Whispers followed me wherever I went, and the judgment was unmistakable. I saw it in the eyes of my classmates, the disapproving glances from their parents, and the strained interactions with teachers. I was no longer just another student, the senior class president; I was that girl.

The shame I carried was unbearable, and there were moments when the weight of it all made me feel like I couldn't go on. I wanted to die. Trauma followed me like a tormenting demon. I couldn't close my eyes without seeing Julie's body in the ditch. PTSD became my companion, showing up in the form of nightmares and panic attacks.

That night didn't just change my life. It shaped every day that came after it. It stole pieces of me and left behind scars that never fully healed. I was left with nothing. No mask. No identity. Just a broken girl drowning in guilt.

Julie never blamed me. Not once. Neither did her parents. We stayed close for a while, figuring out this new reality together. I learned how to help her in and out of a car, how to fold and lift her wheelchair into the trunk. We still laughed sometimes, but it was never the same. Years passed. I moved away. We lost touch, but I never stopped thinking about her.

Mutual friends would tell me bits and pieces. I learned that she moved to Washington D.C. and got a great job. Sadly, her parents divorced. I couldn't help but wonder if it was because of me and what I had done. Every few years, I'd try to find her online. I never did until recently.

Her profile picture stopped me cold. She was smiling, a little boy with strawberry-blonde hair on her lap. A husband next to her. She had built a life, and I was ecstatic to see her with a child.

I'm So Sorry

If my friend or her family ever come across these words, please know there hasn't been a single day that I haven't carried the weight of what happened. The sorrow and the remorse of knowing my choices altered your lives forever are woven into the deepest parts of me. I would give ANYTHING to undo that night, to erase the pain I caused.

From the depths of my soul, I am so sorry.

Reflection

What were you laughing over that you never
gave yourself permission to grieve?

The Lie Behind the Mask

"If I smile instead admitting I'm hurting, they will love me."

The Truth

God sees beyond your smile. You are loved in your
laughter and in your tears.

Psalm 126:5 (NIV)
Those who sow in tears will reap with songs of joy!

CHAPTER SIX

BACKSTAGE NUMB

"A ddiction is a dance with the devil,
       where you lead for a moment but never win."
—Unknown

I had three scholarships, acceptance to Michigan State, and a future full of possibility. But the accident had changed everything. Instead of stepping onto a campus where I could reinvent myself, I was on probation, in a town where my past was inescapable.

At 17, I should have been decorating my dorm room. Instead, I was living upstairs in my boyfriend Craig's father's house, trapped by a sentence I couldn't outrun. Without a license, I had no way to get to school, so I begged Kyle, Craig's father, to let me borrow his car. He would eventually give in with the promise I'd take the backroads. Every mile of that 20-minute drive to Monroe County Community College was torture. I could hear my pulse in my ears; I was so terrified of getting caught.

The Addiction Mask

Robert, one of Craig's closest friends, had moved to Chicago, Illinois, to work for his father's clothing company. He was everything our small-town crowd wasn't. When he invited Craig and I to visit, I jumped at the chance.

Walking into his apartment felt like stepping into a backstage VIP lounge. It smelled of expensive cologne and rainforest incense. The walls pulsed with rap music and everything about it felt indulgent. Then Robert took us on a tour, leading us to a spare bedroom where an entire hydroponic setup gleamed under fluorescent lights. He was so proud of the marijuana crop he was growing.

But that wasn't the only surprise he had to show us. Next came a mirror dusted with multiple lines of cocaine. The sight instantly had my heart beating from what I anticipated next. He took a short straw, snorted a line, and then handed the straw to Craig like it was an appetizer at a party. Craig passed the straw to me. I copied what I saw them do.

The first line of cocaine hit like lightning, electrifying every nerve in my body. The euphoria dissolved everything else that I was dealing with. I was soaring high, engaging in philosophical conversations the entire weekend.

Over the course of 30 years, addiction became the mask that hid trauma and mental illness. It further entangled me in a cycle of fear, depression, and shame. The Addiction Mask conformed to my face quickly. What started as an occasional escape turned into a desperate need. It was just another mask, one that numbed my pain for a moment, only to tighten its grip on me once the high faded.

Craig didn't share my hunger for it; for him, it was just a party drug. But for me, cocaine wasn't just a drug, it was my new identity. It was the thing that made me feel alive, even as it was killing me. Craig and I had been together since I was 16, but I was outgrowing him. He wanted a future in our small town, a predictable life. I wanted more action. So, I found new people.

Drug dealers became my closest friends, and one of them became something more. We had a "working relationship." He kept part of his supply in a safe at my place, and in return, I had unlimited access. But access wasn't free. The arrangement came with expectations.

I remember the night he walked out of my apartment, only to return later with a box of condoms. He tossed them onto my dresser like a pack of gum. They were for us, for whenever he decided it was time to collect his payment.

There were trips, too. Daytona Speedway, weekend getaways, long nights at parties. The Addiction Mask said if I wanted to keep using, I had to play my role. And I wasn't the only one. He brought other women too. I was relieved when he did, because for a moment, his attention shifted to someone else. But the relief never lasted. Eventually, it would be my turn again.

Addiction has a way of stripping you of everything. The drugs in my house made me a target. Break-ins became a regular occurrence, desperate users searching for their next hit. It didn't matter to me that I was using more of the supply than I was supposed to, creating shortages I couldn't afford to explain.

I started dealing drugs myself, thinking it was a way to maintain control over my spiraling life. The only problem was I became my own best customer, constantly dipping into the supply. To cover up the missing product, I tried to "cut" the cocaine, replacing what I used. It was a desperate attempt to stay ahead, but I was always one step behind.

These were the days when the depression was so deep it felt like a bottomless pit. My brain was depleted from the relentless effects of cocaine, and normal life without it didn't exist. The highs and lows consumed me, leaving no room for anything else.

My apartment was filled with empty beer bottles and ashtrays overflowing with cigarette butts.

Nights blurred into mornings as I drank beer and smoked marijuana to try to come down. My body, too exhausted to function. My mind, too wired to sleep. Daylight crept in, and the birds sang their mocking "good morning."

Twenty-First Birthday

A milestone birthday called for a wild night. My best friend and I got dressed up, ready to celebrate like we were untouchable. She knew how to turn heads—tight dress, high heels, confidence that filled a room. I, on the other hand, was always half-pretending.

We climbed into my white Mitsubishi Eclipse and headed to an upscale club downriver in Detroit. The bass shook the walls, the lights blurred, and the drinks kept coming. "Sex on the Beach" shots lined the table. We danced, laughed, and soaked up all the attention.

When it was time to leave, she argued with me. "Are you sure you're good to drive?"

I waved her off. "I'm fine. I know my car better than anyone."

The truth? I wasn't fine. But denial was my constant companion.

I never made it to the highway.

The sound of metal grinding against the guardrail was distant, like it belonged to another life. My first clear thought came when I saw my friend standing outside the wreck, screaming through tears.

"What the hell is wrong with you?" she cried. "I have kids!"

Then came the flashing lights—police, paramedics, a tow truck. Somehow, miraculously, we were both fine. Not a single scratch. I should've been on my knees thanking God, but I was too numb to feel anything.

In the back of the cop car, one officer turned toward us. "Either of you carrying any drugs?"

Her wide eyes met mine. *You better tell them.*

I reluctantly answered, "Yeah. I have some."

I handed over the drugs I was holding to sell but kept my personal stash tucked away. A junkie move. To my shock, they didn't arrest us. They just dropped us off at a Denny's and said, "Call a cab."

The cab ride home was brutal. My friend stared out the window, silent at first, then exploded.

"You're a horrible person," she snapped. "You could've killed me. I swear to God, I'll never speak to you again."

I didn't argue. She was right.

The driver dropped her off first, then drove another twenty miles to my boyfriend's place downtown. I threw up in the back seat, couldn't pay, and stumbled to his door—half-hoping he was alone, half-expecting to find someone else there.

Another close call. Another brush with death. Another miracle I didn't deserve.

I should've seen it as a wake-up call, but I was still too blind to notice the mercy in it.

The Mask of Illusion

After earning my Associate of Science degree, I took an office job working for three construction company owners. I learned the ins and outs of Accounts Payable, Accounts Receivable, Payroll, and more. I was making more money than I ever had, legally. Then one day, a friend casually mentioned how much she was making as an exotic dancer.

The idea planted itself in my mind and wouldn't let go. It wasn't just about the money—though the thought of making more in a single night than I did in weeks at my office job was tempting. It was about the illusion of control. The belief that I could reclaim power over my life by using the one thing I thought I still had to offer: my body. That's how I stepped into my next mask, the Mask of Illusion.

I walked into the club for the first time. The lights were dim, casting a hazy glow over the room. The bass from the music thrummed through my chest. She introduced me to the manager and within minutes, I was being shown to the dressing room. As I slipped into the costume I had brought, I watched the other dancers change with boldness and confidence. I could feel my heart pounding in my ears. I wasn't sure if it was fear or excitement. Maybe both.

Taking the stage as "Diamond," I felt a strange mixture of terror and adrenaline. The first time, I needed a few drinks to work up the nerve. Shots of whiskey became my armor, dulling the sharp edges of fear, just enough to let me walk under the bright lights onto the stage.

"Dancing Queen" blasted through the club as cheers erupted around me. For a fleeting moment, the cash raining down felt like validation.

The money I earned dancing trumped what I was making in my office job, and the rush of it was intoxicating in its own right. But the Mask of Illusion couldn't hold the act together forever.

The glamour quickly faded. Beneath the lights and music, I was still the same broken woman I'd always been, trading pieces of myself for an illusion of freedom. Each night, as the applause died down and the cash was counted, the emptiness crept back in. I'd sit in the dressing room, surrounded by other dancers laughing and chatting as they peeled off their costumes, and I'd feel utterly alone.

The shame and self-loathing were unbearable. Sweaty from dancing, scents of men's cologne clinging to me from lap dances, I'd head home to a dark room that awaited me. It was always the same: an apartment littered with empty beer bottles and ashtrays overflowing with cigarette butts. I'd drink myself into a stupor, trying to silence the voices in my head that told me I was unworthy of anything better.

The same darkness that had followed me through my addiction was waiting for me in the shadows of the club. The bright lights couldn't hide it, and the cash couldn't buy it away. The stage might have been an escape, but it was really just another cage.

Addiction wasn't just about the drugs or the money or the choices I made. It was about the way I had come to see myself as unworthy of love, of respect, of anything good. I wasn't just a slave to the drugs. I was a slave to the belief that I didn't deserve anything better.

Financially depleted and morally bankrupt, I became a master manipulator. I lied, I stole, I exploited anyone who dared to care about me. Every relationship was a transaction, every interaction a chance to take what I needed to keep my addiction alive. But no matter how hard I tried to fill the void, it only grew deeper. The claws of addiction weren't just in my body; they were in my soul.

The Mask of Illusion was seductive. It convinced me that I was in control, that I had reclaimed my power. The Mask of Addiction tightened its grip, whispering that I needed more money, more substances to keep the illusion alive. With every drink, every line of cocaine, every dollar tucked into my costume, I buried myself deeper into a life that wasn't mine.

Hope is on the Horizon

The masks gave me an identity I thought I controlled. But over time, I began to realize I wasn't wearing the masks anymore. The masks were wearing me. I wore them everywhere: into every relationship, every conversation, and I was left with nothing but the hollow shell of who I used to be.

I see now how tightly I was bound, how desperately I clung to anything that promised relief from the pain. But even in my darkest moments, there was a part of me that longed for freedom. That longing would one day become the spark that saved me. For now, though, I was trapped, sinking deeper with every choice I made. Beneath the wreckage, something was stirring. A buried belief that maybe I wasn't meant to stay trapped forever.

A Truth to Behold

Perhaps you can relate to some of my experiences. Maybe you've worn masks of your own, playing roles that kept you safe but never truly free. Maybe you've chased after things that numbed the pain but never healed it. You might have felt the pressure to fit in or the desperation to feel loved and wanted, even if it meant making choices you later regretted.

If you've ever felt that emptiness inside or chased after something to fill the void, know that you're not alone. It's easy to get lost when you're trying to escape pain or find comfort, but acknowledging these feelings is the first step toward healing. If you see yourself in my story, I hope that vision helps you realize that change is possible and that it's never too late to find a different path.

Reflection

The Mask of Numbness dulled every pain of life you didn't want to feel.
Under its mask, pain became bearable because you didn't feel anything
fully—not the highs, not the lows.
What pain did the Mask of Addiction help you hide?
What feelings did the Mask of Numbness help you not to feel?

The Lie Behind the Mask

"Escaping reality is freedom."

The Truth

You were made to live free and fully present with hope, without hiding
behind the Mask of Numbness.

Isaiah 41:10 (NKJV)
Fear not, for I am with you; Be not dismayed, for I am your God.
I will strengthen you,
Yes, I will help you, I will uphold you with My righteous right hand.

CHAPTER SEVEN

THE MASQUERADE TURNS DEADLY

"The more you try to control something, the more it controls you."

—Unknown

Desperate for a fresh start and eager to leave my past behind, I decided to head to Alabama after a brief fling with a one-night stand. I threw my belongings into a borrowed car and headed for Alabama, convinced a new city could rewrite my story. I thought, "This is it! I'm going to start my life over where no one knows who I am."

But running wasn't enough. I could change my location, my surroundings, even my name if I wanted to, but I was still wearing the same mask. The Mask of Escape. The thing with masks is that they don't erase what's underneath. No matter how many of them I put on, no matter what I changed, I took myself with me and that's what the problem was.

Shortly after settling in Tuscaloosa, I linked up with a girl, Lucy, who lived like I did—fast, reckless, and always chasing the next high. She introduced me to a new kind of escape, one that came with a needle and a line. Shooting up cocaine. Snorting heroin. It made me sick, it scared me, but I did it anyway. By this point, I didn't care what happened to me.

The burn in my nose hadn't even faded before the rush hit me like a freight train. My vision blurred, my body went limp, and the room started spinning. Distant voices cut through the haze.

"Get her up! Get her up!"

Hands gripped my arms, dragging me toward the bathroom. My knees hit the cold tile as I collapsed in front of the toilet. Then came the heaving, my body rejecting the poison I had just forced into it. I clung to the rim of the bowl, shaking. I had just crossed another line I could never uncross.

Instead of running away or simply stopping, I wiped my mouth, stumbled to my feet, and did it all over again. The rest of the night dissolved into a haze of pounding music, and hands pulling me in every direction. I performed like a puppet, numb and detached, passed like a rag doll from one grasp to another.

The echoes of that night claw at me, a nightmare that never truly fades.

Dancing With the Illusion

Lucy introduced me to her dealer who quickly took a keen interest in me. It was a pattern. I was fresh bait, an easy target for those who would use me to feed their own addictions. But this guy felt different, at least at first. We bonded over our love for Prince, spending hours listening to his music.

He almost seemed protective, warning me against touching his supply. For a brief moment, I believed he had my best interests at heart. Addiction doesn't care about good intentions. The craving always wins. I didn't know how to shoot up, but that changed fast.

Another girl, the kind born into privilege, would pull up in her sleek two-seater BMW, desperate for a fix. One night, she took me into a back room and showed me how to hook her up. It didn't take long before I was doing it myself, the needle slipping under my skin, delivering a rush

I couldn't have prepared for. I had crossed another line, and again, there was no going back.

Chasing Escape to Homelessness

The guy who had invited me down—a one-night stand I foolishly thought could turn into something meaningful—was never into the hard stuff, just smoking weed. But once he and his buddies burned through my entire stash, he discarded me without hesitation, using my association with Lucy as an excuse to push me away. It was humiliating.

My life in Alabama spiraled fast. Every high was just another attempt to keep the masquerade going; to keep pretending I had control. I had become a ghost in my own story, drifting through scenes I didn't recognize, wearing a mask I did not know how to remove.

By this time, my connection with my family was practically nonexistent, so with nowhere to go, I bounced around until I wore out my welcome and found myself completely homeless, living out of my car. I had no money, no plan, and no one to turn to. Desperation set in as I sold whatever I could just to scrape together enough money for gas. With nothing left but the clothes on my back, I turned the car north and started the long drive back to Michigan, hoping for some kind of refuge at the end of the road.

The truth was, I needed healing. Not hiding.

Reflection

What pain have you tried to outrun,
only to find it chasing you wherever you go?

The Lie Behind the Mask

"Pain is unbearable, so I must distract, numb, or run from it."

The Truth

Running doesn't bring freedom.
Facing the pain is the beginning of healing.

Psalms 94:19 (NLT)
When doubts filled my mind,
your comfort gave me renewed hope and cheer.

Scan to begin your unmasking journey
and step into freedom from denial.

ACT II

The Stage Crumbles. The Soul Awakens

Act II invites you into the raw moments where the walls begin to crumble and the masks fall away. Here, grief crashes in, crises emerge, and the ache of survival becomes undeniable. But within the darkness, a flicker of hope appears—spiritual shifts, inner healing, and the first steps toward a new identity. This act is about breaking down to break through, facing pain head-on, and starting to rewrite the script of a life once lived in shadows.

CHAPTER EIGHT

INTERMISSION: THE PAUSE OF TRUTH

"She stood in the storm, and when the wind did not blow her way, she adjusted her sails."
—Elizabeth Edwards

After everything I've shared so far, I want to take a moment to look back, with the clarity I now have. My choices weren't just impulsive or reckless; they were deeply influenced by an internal struggle. One I couldn't always recognize or articulate. At the time, I thought I was just lost or making bad decisions, but I now see that I was fighting a battle I didn't fully understand.

To cope with the constant emotional turmoil, I developed a range of behaviors. I engaged in dangerous and risky behaviors and formed destructive relationships with individuals who were themselves entrenched in addiction. This pattern exposed me to a realm of harmful influences, including drug dealers and other addicts. The need to sustain my addiction led me to exploit and manipulate those around me, further isolating myself from anyone safe.

Financial ruin and moral decay were inevitable consequences of these choices. Coping became a means of survival in a world that felt increasingly out of control. Reflecting on these experiences, it is clear that there was a greater force at work which perpetuated a cycle of torment and utter destruction.

Revealing My Role in the Story

Now that I've said all of this, I feel the need to separate a few things because understanding them clearly helped me heal: Yes, I made bad choices. No one forced me to live recklessly. Those decisions were mine, shaped by my own will—yet also influenced by so many layers I didn't fully understand at the time. The environment I was raised in, the biological traits I inherited, the spiritual atmosphere I was under, and the trauma that ran like an undercurrent through my family line.

This is where the concept of epigenetics started to make sense to me. In simple terms, epigenetics is the study of how our environment and experiences can turn on or off certain genes. That means trauma, addiction, abuse, and even emotional neglect from generations before us can literally impact how our bodies and minds' function, without changing our DNA itself. It's like certain switches were flipped on in me long before I had the language to understand what I was battling.

But even with that knowledge, I'm not making excuses. I'm just telling the truth. Those generational wounds, those biological and spiritual factors positioned me to make destructive choices, but they didn't force me to. My soul—my mind, my emotions, and especially my will, was still mine. I partnered with darkness.

I walked straight into every demonic trap laid before me, knocking on doors that should have stayed shut. I didn't stumble into bondage: I often ran headfirst. Being wired the way I was, with a sensitive nature, deep emotional wounds, and a hunger for connection, made it even harder to choose well. But I still had the power of choice. And every decision had a consequence, whether I understood it in the moment or not.

What I'm learning now, and what I pray you can receive too, is that awareness is not the same as an excuse or self-pity. I couldn't control what others did to me. I couldn't change my genetics, my upbringing, or the spiritual battles assigned to my bloodline. But I was and am responsible for my responses and healing.

You are not your trauma.

You are not your addiction.

You are not the curse that ran through your bloodline.

Owning that truth doesn't bring shame. It brings freedom. You can close the doors you once opened. You can renounce the lies you believed. You can be healed: spirit, soul, and body.

Hope in the Depths

When change feels out of reach and disappointment lingers, it's easy to believe the lie that things will never get better. I've believed that lie, fought against it, and nearly let it consume me. But just because hope feels distant doesn't mean it's gone.

There is a time for mourning, but that means joy is promised on the other side. It's not wishful thinking. It's the deep assurance that the darkness will not last forever. I have walked through shadows, believing I would never see the light again, but hope kept whispering, "keep going."

I saw that hope in my mother, my aunt, and unexpected souls who crossed my path like hope dealers, instead of drug dealers. People carrying something powerful, declaring into the atmosphere, "You are not done yet." The darkness may roar like a lion, but it is never victorious. Every time, light overpowers it.

A Truth to Behold

Hope is relentless. Even if all you have left is a small ember buried beneath the ashes, it is enough. Hold onto it. Because that flicker of hope is the evidence that your story is far from over.

So today, I stand as a hope dealer, speaking life into the places that feel barren and fanning that ember inside you into a roaring flame. I declare that hopelessness will not have the final word over your life. You were not made to stay in the pit, to be buried under the weight of your past, your pain, or your mistakes. You were made to rise.

Let hope uproot the lies that say you're too far gone. You are not forgotten. You are not abandoned. There is a way forward, and step by step, you will walk into the fullness of it. The same light that shattered my darkness is breaking through for you now. So, lift your head, breathe deep, and keep moving.

Hope is now!

Reflection

What agreements have you made in the dark that God is now inviting you to break in the light?

The Lie Behind the Mask

"Isolating myself keeps me safe from the disappointment from others."

The Truth

Hope exposes the lie that darkness is your only shelter.

John 1:5 (NIV)
The light shines in the darkness, and the darkness has not overcome it.

CHAPTER NINE

A DANCE WITH FATE

"When God writes your story, even the detours have purpose."
—Unknown

Returning to Michigan felt less like a fresh start and more like drifting back into a familiar fog. At 25, I was drained—mentally, emotionally, and spiritually. I had no dreams, no real plans, and no concern for my own survival.

Addiction doesn't let go so easily. The hunger for cocaine still clutched onto me, even as I tried to settle into something resembling stability. I told myself I could stay clean, that maybe this time would be different. But deep down, I knew the battle wasn't over.

It didn't take long until I was introduced to another dealer. Soon, he was picking me up to "party." We would meet at motels where I was first introduced to smoking crack cocaine. I became bait, traded for crack cocaine. My life became consumed with nothing but getting high. I had lost all sense of purpose. I didn't care if I lived another day.

I found myself a place to stay in Monroe, Michigan, staying with a friend I met through my sister. The arrangement was straightforward. He offered a warm bed to share and a steady supply of marijuana. But my craving for the high that cocaine provided was still strong, and he made it clear that he wasn't into that and wouldn't support my habit.

I returned to my usual routine, seeking people in the city who could 'hook me up' with the right connections. Before long, I found myself at a party in someone's basement, surrounded by plenty of cocaine.

Word quickly traveled back to the guy I was staying with that I'd been partying on the "wrong side of the tracks". He must have thought we had something more serious going on because he gave me an ultimatum: either stop hanging out with those people or find somewhere else to live.

I realized I couldn't keep up my habit or keep stringing him along any longer—so I left. It wasn't working in my favor anymore. After all, it was ultimately about my own selfish addiction and my needs. Once again, I found myself with no options, exchanging my body to find a way to get high and have a place to stay.

A Dance with Fate

I found a job as a server at a local fine dining Italian restaurant. The tips were fantastic, and I even got to pick up extra hours working for their catering business and serving at private parties.

One night while I was working at the restaurant, a friend I hadn't seen in a while came in for dinner. We reconnected, and he invited me to go out and "party" with him after my shift. It was a slow weeknight with nothing else going on, so I agreed to have him swing by after closing to pick me up.

We headed downriver to a club just south of Detroit called *Hip Shakers*. Before even going inside, we spent time in his truck, snorting 'gaggers': huge lines of coke that were so intense they'd make you gag.

Inside the club, the music pulsed through the air like a heartbeat, while the strobe lights sliced through the dark. The high from the cocaine made everything feel amplified, the rhythm of the music blending with the rush in my veins. But it never lasted long enough. Repeatedly, I went outside, back in the truck, chasing the high.

At one point in the night, I strutted over to the DJ booth to request a song by The Gap Band and ended up near a group of guys hanging out by the DJ. Most of them were smoking, so I asked to bum a cigarette. None of them had my usual menthols—except for the one African

American guy sitting quietly on a stool. I boldly asked him for one, and he handed it over with no hesitation.

Later in the night, just before closing, the DJ started playing a couple of slow songs to wind things down. I maneuvered my way through the crowd back to the guy I had bummed the cigarette from. He was still sitting on that stool. Feeling a surge of boldness, I walked up to him and asked his name, quickly following it up with, "Do you want to dance?"

He smiled and said, "My name's Aaron."

As he stood, towering over me, I couldn't help but blurt out, "Wow! You're so tall!" He smiled and told me he was six-foot-four, exactly a foot taller than me. Luckily, I had on my brown leather boots with heels, giving me a little boost!

As we danced to Marvin Gaye's, "Let's Get It On," time felt suspended. I didn't know it then, but I was dancing toward a moment that would alter everything. Before we said goodbye that night, I gave him my beeper number. We arranged to meet later that week.

I remember thinking, "This guy is really articulate, intelligent, and polite." Still, I couldn't shake the feeling that he might be more my sister's type, and I even wondered if I should introduce them.

It didn't take long before I changed my mind, realizing I wanted to keep getting to know him for myself. Something about him drew me in, and the idea of handing him off to anyone else quickly faded away.

I was yearning for a fresh start, desperate for a reason to live. I felt a deep longing for connection and a place to belong. I moved in with Aaron and his roommates, and things moved quickly. Before I knew it—within a month—I was pregnant!

In the quiet corners of my soul, I knew neither of us had tried to prevent it. It was wordless, but it was intentional. He was sober, and I was slightly buzzed, but not enough for either of us to pretend we didn't know what we were doing.

Aaron had told me he was legally separated from his wife, who lived in Ohio with their three young daughters. He would occasionally visit, returning with the faint crumbs of his kid's childhood—traces of the youngest girl's tiny hands on his shirt.

One afternoon, while sitting outside the apartment in my parked car, he shared another truth that took me by surprise: the woman who lived in Ohio wasn't his first wife—he had two older sons from a previous relationship. The woman he was separated from then was his second wife.

A baby was coming and somehow, amidst the uncertainty, it felt like this was meant to be.

The Delusion of Denial

I wish I could tell you that discovering I was pregnant changed everything. But addiction doesn't bow easily. I was still using marijuana regularly, hiding it from him since he was firmly against it. Most nights after work, I'd stop by the corner store to grab a 24-oz can of beer, drinking on the drive home. It was a chaotic dance of avoidance where I grappled with the truth of my pregnancy and refusing to conform to his demands. He finally decided to leave for Fort Wayne, Indiana, in pursuit of a job his friends had lined up.

I was left there pregnant and alone.

I was abandoned in an apartment with his former roommates. It didn't take long for me to reconnect with the crack dealer from Toledo, Ohio, picking up our "relationship" right where we had left off. We frequented dark clubs with back entrances, where the air was thick with the buzz of gambling, drug deals, strippers, and prostitutes. Sometimes, he would drop me off at a rundown motel or leave me at the home of an addict while he tended to his "business."

In that haze of chaos, I somehow managed to deny my pregnancy, convincing him to let me take a hit from the crack pipe. If that didn't work, I'd plead with him to roll a small piece of rock into a joint. Each hit was a frantic attempt to escape the reality I was avoiding, as I clung to fleeting moments of oblivion.

One of my roommates kept Aaron updated on everything I was doing, and any hope of reconciliation slipped away. He moved on quickly, diving into a new relationship and getting an apartment for the two of them.

Five months pregnant, I applied for state benefits and secured a spot in Section 8 Housing. This change forced me to hold down a part-time job, which brought stability to my life for the first time in ages.

I felt an overwhelming wave of shame crashing over me, being pregnant and unwed. The added complexity of the baby's father being African American deepened the fear of judgment and rejection I anticipated from my predominantly Caucasian community. The thought of telling my parents filled me with dread. My mother held tightly to Christian values that insisted on marriage before sex and babies, while my father's disappointment about my life's choices loomed large. I feared his reactions and the unspoken shame I was bringing to our family.

Praying to God felt like a desperate grasp for something I hadn't touched in years. I hadn't prayed or even thought about God since I was 16, following the car accident that shook my life to its core.

August in Michigan felt unbearable with no air conditioning, making sleep nearly impossible. The incessant barking of a dog echoed through the night, only adding to my misery.

In the darkness, consumed by depression, I lay awake, begging God to bring the baby's father back into my life. I promised that if He did, I would finally live my life the right way, as if my future hinged entirely on this one man returning to me. It wasn't the first deal I'd tried to strike with God, nor would it be the last.

Birth of a New Identity and Purpose

What happened inside of me during those tumultuous months rescued me from the path I had been living on. By the grace of God, my angel baby girl was born healthy. I truly believe her arrival saved my life!

I still felt a deep sadness and disappointment that her father didn't show up for the birth, yet the rush of joy I experienced was so overwhelming that it overshadowed my sadness entirely. I chose not to find out the gender of our baby beforehand. So, when I called to share the news that we had a girl, hearing his girlfriend answer the phone hit me like a blow. His first response was, "Another girl?"

Despite his reaction, the overwhelming delight of giving birth, surrounded by my mom, aunt, and two sisters, eclipsed the knife-like pain in my heart.

Within days of her birth, my prayers were answered! Aaron came to visit us and meet our daughter. I was struck by how he seemed to know how to care for a newborn better than I did. After asking his girlfriend to leave, he offered for us to move in with him. Tears of joy streamed down my face as I eagerly accepted his offer, clinging to the hope of a fresh start and ready to embrace the opportunity to build a new life together in Indiana.

It was around this time that I also learned that Aaron's divorce from his second wife had been finalized in October, just before our daughter was born in November. I didn't hesitate to give her his last name. His name was missing from her birth certificate, but after her birth, we reconciled the paperwork when he signed an affidavit declaring paternity.

Becoming a new mom filled my life with an overwhelming joy I had never experienced before! It gave me the strength to walk away from the heavy drugs that consumed me—no more cocaine, heroin, crack, or meth. I often reflect on the stark contrast between where I am now and where I could have ended up. Without that moment of grace, I might have faced death, imprisonment, or the unbearable heartbreak of losing my child.

For anyone who has walked a similar path, my heart bleeds for you. It's never too late to reclaim your life from the death grip of addiction.

Reflection

What if your most painful chapter was actually
the prologue to your redemption?

The Lie Behind the Mask

"The consequences that I'm facing are a punishment to me.
I'm deserving of these hardships."

The Truth

Redemption often enters through unexpected doors.

Isaiah 44:22 (NKJV)
I have blotted out, like a thick cloud, your transgressions,
And like a cloud, your sins.
Return to Me, for I have redeemed you."

CHAPTER TEN

CURTAINS RISE ON A NEW LIFE

"We are all broken, that's how the light gets in."

—Ernest Hemingway

As we settled into our new apartment in Fort Wayne, Indiana, I fully embraced the role of being a mom. Life felt simple but sweet. One of the promises Aaron made was to take care of us.

He worked afternoons at the foundry, and our mornings became a ritual. I'd wake early to cook him breakfast, kiss him goodbye as he left, and then dive into my day. One of my favorite parts of the day was clipping coupons and checking competitor ads, figuring out how much I could save on groceries. Every bit helped. My favorite store even had a "New Mom's" parking spot near the front, a small kindness that made those early days feel a little lighter.

This fresh start was nothing like the life I'd known over the past decade. I remember one cool spring morning, pushing my daughter in her stroller, along the quiet sidewalks of the neighborhood near our third-floor apartment. With each step, something started to shift. I felt good. Waves of joy flooded my mind and body. A sense of peace was finally showing up in my life.

Double Blessing

Just as I was starting to settle into life as a new mom, another shock wrecked me. I was pregnant again, only four months after having my daughter! I remember staring at the positive test in disbelief, sitting at the top of the stairwell with one of Aaron's Newport 100s in my hand. Numb, I couldn't believe what I saw.

Our one-bedroom apartment already felt cramped, with a crib squeezed into the corner of our room and baby gear covering every spare inch. I was still nursing my daughter and beginning to find a rhythm—and now another baby was on the way. Being a single, unwed mother settled heavily on me. Aaron and I had talked about marriage for "someday," but suddenly I needed "someday" to be now.

Within a few weeks, we made arrangements for a small ceremony. We invited my family and a couple of close friends to the local botanical gardens. As we stood in front of the magistrate, I didn't try to hide the pregnancy. I figured maybe my parents would feel better seeing us take this step. But even in that moment—standing there with people who loved us—I still felt a quiet shame I couldn't shake.

One of the most meaningful moments from our wedding day was when my mom offered me her own wedding dress. A friend of mine made a few changes to make it fit over my five-month pregnant belly, transforming it into something that felt like mine. There was a full-circle moment in that.

My mom wore the same dress when she was 17, and five months pregnant with me. The difference was, back then, she and my dad kept it a secret. Pregnancy before marriage carried a deeper shame in her generation. Or did it?

Our wedding day was small, intimate, and yet filled with signifi-cance. It wasn't the lavish celebration I had once imagined, but it was perfect. My family, a few close friends, and the small group that had supported us along the way gathered to witness this holy moment.

What made the day even more special was my dad walking me down the aisle. As he took my arm and led me toward Aaron, I could feel a weight of shame lifting off my shoulders. I wasn't alone anymore. We had faced so much uncertainty up to that point, and being able to stand before the people who mattered most to us felt like a powerful turning point. The path ahead still had its challenges, but I felt ready to build something new.

The Key to a New Chapter

Our one-bedroom apartment felt smaller with each passing day as we anticipated the arrival of our second baby. Desperate for more space, I urged Aaron to take the next step and find us a home for our growing family. I helped him fill out a mortgage application, and to our surprise, he was approved.

We quickly found a perfect three-bedroom house in a quiet neighborhood, with sidewalks for a nice stroll and a small park nearby. It felt like a breath of fresh air, the start of something hopeful and new.

Within the first few months in our new home, life got busy fast. Our precious son, Aaron II, who we nicknamed "Ronny", was born. I loved the whirlwind of caring for two little ones; finding joy in the routines and organizing each room as if I were endlessly nesting. That time was filled with excitement and purpose, but eventually, the newness faded.

Aaron and I shared one important thing in common: we were both raised with a belief in God. His grandfather had been a Baptist preacher. Aaron spent his childhood attending church whenever the doors were open. For me, motherhood started to shift things. I began thinking about my children's future and how I wanted to raise them with the same values I had been taught.

As the cracks in our marriage started to show, we both agreed we needed something more. We talked about visiting churches, hoping maybe it would help us. One of Aaron's coworkers kept inviting him to his church, so we finally decided to check it out. They met in a movie theater, and while everyone was warm and welcoming, we just didn't quite connect with the atmosphere.

Divine Encounter at the Olive Garden

Aaron's three daughters were still living a couple hours away in Ohio. On his oldest daughter's 10th birthday, she came to visit, and we took her out to eat at Olive Garden. The place was packed. We stood in the lobby waiting to be seated, and Ronny—just one month old—was starting to fuss. I needed to find a quiet spot to nurse. I went to check the bathroom, hoping maybe there'd be a chair.

As I walked in, a lady noticed me right away and asked, "Are you looking for a place to nurse your baby?" "Yes," I said. She kindly offered to help find a chair. A few minutes later, our table was ready. I thanked her, and we went to our seat, assuming that was the last I'd see of her. But partway through our meal, she came by to introduce herself. She handed us a card from her church, *New Hope Worship Center*, and invited us to visit. That's when I found out she was the pastor's wife.

I pinned the church card to my corkboard, where it stayed untouched for weeks. At 27, with two babies under two, stuck in a deep depression, I was trying to wear the Good Wife Mask. I felt a pull to check out the church. I finally worked up the courage to go alone to a Tuesday night Bible study.

As I pulled into the parking lot, I saw a stream of women walking in, wearing skirts and dresses. Meanwhile, I sat there in my favorite purple sweats, hair barely brushed. I thought about turning around. The sign said, "Come as you are," but maybe I had taken that too literally. Still, I went in.

I slipped quietly into the back row, hoping not to be noticed. That didn't work. Several ladies came over right away to introduce themselves and welcome me. At the end of the service, Sister Bower, the pastor's wife, greeted me with such warmth and excitement. She remembered me from Olive Garden and asked me to fill out a connect card so she could follow up.

I went back that Sunday morning for a full service. The worship and energy in the building hit something in me, reminding me of being a little girl going to church with my mom. Something was stirring deep within me.

In the weeks that followed, different women from the church would visit me at home, bringing cookies, flowers, and Veggie Tales videos for the kids. The most surprising gesture came on Easter weekend. We had just gotten back from visiting our family in Michigan, and there on our porch was a homemade lamb-shaped cake, and a note from Sister Bower. That moment wrecked me. Nobody had ever loved me like that without wanting something in return.

Scene Change: From Mask to Mercy

On May 6, 2001, I showed up for a Sunday night service. An older woman evangelist was preaching, pacing the stage, fiery and full of passion. By the end of her message, she gave an invitation for anyone needing prayer to come forward. Without hesitation, my heart pounding, I rushed to the altar.

Women gathered around me, praying in tongues and encouraging me to receive my own prayer language. I didn't question it. I just knew I wanted the "new life" the evangelist spoke of. As I opened my mouth to pray, I felt an overwhelming release of emotion. I cried hard—like something deep was being broken off. Then someone asked, "Do you want to be water-baptized?" Without a second thought, I said, "Yes!"

I changed into a gown and stepped into the baptistry. Pastor Bower lowered me into the water, and when I came back up, something happened. I felt this power surge through me. My mouth started moving in an unknown language I'd never heard before. It wasn't something I forced. It just came.

In that miraculous moment—the guilt, the shame, the years of pain—it all lifted. Everything looked brighter and more vibrant. I'd just stepped into a whole new life.

I felt high!
I felt clean!
I felt free!

The Truth

Real healing doesn't come from performance or perfection. It comes
when God calls you to step into His light.

Isaiah 60:1 (NKJV)
Arise, shine; For your light has come!
And the glory of the Lord is risen upon you.

Scan to be led in a prayer to receive the gift of salvation.

CHAPTER ELEVEN

THE DANCE OF DEVOTION

"**R**emember, in the depth and even agony of despondency, that very shortly you are to feel well again."
—Abraham Lincoln

After my born-again experience, something shifted deep inside. I began reading my Bible and suddenly, the words weren't just text. It was as if they came alive and jumped off the page into my heart and mind. I began journaling, as if I was speaking directly to God, bearing my heart and soul. It felt odd at first, but the release I experienced by putting pen to paper was a time I looked forward to. Now, as I write this memoir, it's incredible to be pouring over my journals from the past 24 years, gleaning from my experience. I see the thread of God's faithfulness in every season.

The road ahead was still blurry, but I knew one thing for sure: I wasn't walking it alone anymore. The Word became my anchor and illuminated each step on my path forward.

Winter's Weight

When Ronny was ready to wean, a wave of unexpected darkness hit. It was February—cold, gray, and unrelenting. I slipped into a deep depression; a place I thought I'd left behind. Yet here it was again, familiar and heavy, pulling me down when I least expected it. I could barely manage to take a shower, let alone care for my children.

Most days, I did the bare minimum, retreating to my bed whenever I could. Naptime became the highlight of my day, a chance to crawl back into bed and escape for a while.

People at church started to notice. I couldn't fake it like I used to. One young woman came over regularly to help with dishes and cleaning, trying to quietly offer what I couldn't ask for. Everyone assumed it was postpartum depression or seasonal affective disorder—or maybe both.

My husband, though concerned, didn't understand what I was going through. He urged me to snap out of it and get back to normal. But I couldn't. In my search for something that could ease the pain, I turned to something I knew, marijuana. The old crutch that helped me cope before, even if just for a moment.

Aaron didn't regularly attend church with us. And that hurt more than I let on. It felt so familiar to my experience growing up when my mom would take us all to church and dad stayed home. We were like two travelers carrying heavy suitcases, filled with our unspoken histories and painful memories.

We barely knew each other. We had a whirlwind romance of only a month before we were swept into the deep waters of parenthood. In between, we quickly married with two babies just 14 months apart. My days were blurred by depression and the overwhelming demands of caring for them.

As the days went on, the distance between us seemed to grow. Money was tight, so I decided to look for a part-time job that would fit around Aaron's day shift, even though he didn't want me working outside the home. I wanted to earn a little extra money, and I felt it was necessary for my sanity. I was hired at IHOP as a server, working four nights a week over the weekend. My shifts ran from 10 p.m. to 6 a.m., and then I'd rush home to nurse Ronny so Aaron could leave for work at the foundry. I'd feed the baby; he'd drift back to sleep, and I'd collapse for a few hours—only to be woken by Ashlee two to three hours later. It was brutal to rise after such short rest, but I pushed through, keeping my focus on getting both children to their next nap so I could go to sleep again. There were moments when we smiled, when we laughed. But mostly, we just passed each other like strangers.

A Decision That Shattered Us

Aaron decided to quit his job and head to Arizona to "clear his head." The separation became painfully real. I honestly think he didn't want to go, but I didn't encourage him to stay either. Truth is, I offered to help him pack. Thankfully, his dad, Jesse, had recently moved to Fort Wayne and stepped in to help me with the children.

One day, while calling Jesse to check in on the kids, I'll never forget hearing Ronny, just two and a half, in his tiny voice ask, "Is Daddy's heart broken?"

Three days after Aaron left, I found out my employer was planning to shut down their location. Just like that, I was jobless and alone with two toddlers. Panic set in. I heard about an opening at a local restaurant and immediately started filling out the application online. While I was online, another listing caught my eye. I didn't fully understand what the position entailed. I applied anyway, not even bothering to upload a resume.

To my surprise, the second opportunity led to a call for an interview, while the restaurant never got back to me. I was drowning in uncertainty about being a single parent with a single income, torn between wanting to stay home full-time and the need to find stable work. A second interview came quicker than I expected, leaving me almost hoping they wouldn't make an offer. How would I manage a full-time job and raise my children alone? But life rarely waits for you to feel ready.

A few days later, a FedEx envelope arrived at my door with a formal job offer from General Electric's Legacy Motors business. I had been offered an associate professional position as an Inside Sales Representative—a salary higher than I had ever earned before. I felt unprepared, overwhelmed even, but I accepted it anyway. This was the opportunity I needed to support my family and move forward.

There was no doubt in my mind that I had been given uncommon favor to be offered this position. This was the door that opened—and it would remain a part of my life for the next 13 years.

Yearning for Family

Aaron stayed away for two months. Anytime I asked where he was staying or who he was with, I was met with a wall of anger. His evasiveness left me even more anxious, tangled up in fears I couldn't voice. I was less worried about myself and more terrified that our kids would grow up being abandoned by their father.

I couldn't even say I liked the woman staring back at me in the mirror. Love her? Not a chance. I was too busy wearing the Devoted Wife Mask, pretending to have it all together while inside, I was falling apart. That reflection felt like a stranger. I had rehearsed the role so long, I didn't know how to step off stage.

As our daughter's fourth birthday came closer, I swallowed my pride and begged Aaron to come home. I stuffed down the questions that might upset him and told myself this was what a loyal wife did. I just wanted our family whole even if it meant pretending everything was fine.

With the kids strapped in the backseat, I drove to the Greyhound station, trying to steady the storm of emotions inside me. When Aaron stepped off the bus, I focused on the joy of his return, even as tension lingered in the silence between us.

Reflection

Have you ever confused loyalty with love—and lost yourself in the performance of devotion?

The Lie Behind the Mask

"In order to fully prove my devotion,
my wants and needs need to disappear."

The Truth

Faithfulness to another should never require betrayal of your own soul.

Matthew 16:26 (NKJV)
For what profit is it to a man if he gains the whole world, and loses his own soul? Or what will a man give in exchange for his soul?

CHAPTER TWELVE

EXIT OF THE DEVOTED WIFE

"Sometimes the only way to see yourself clearly is to watch everything fall apart."
—Unknown

Two months after Aaron came home, he was still job hunting. I was the only one bringing in income. Most evenings, he and his dad sat in separate rooms, watching the same show on different TVs. I began to resent it—working all day and still having to ask them to sit together as they watched the same thing.

Then one night, after church, I snapped. I told Aaron and Jesse that maybe I'd like to sit on the couch and relax. The argument escalated quickly, and then he turned physical against me. Jesse disappeared to his room while it happened and shut the door. I bolted outside, barefoot in the snow, pounding on a neighbor's door for help. They didn't answer.

I made my way around the back, grabbed the phone, and dialed 911. The police came and questioned us both. Then they cuffed Aaron and took him to jail. Ronny stood at the door, crying, "I want my daddy back!" When it came time for court, I chose to press charges. I was shocked to realize I was one of the few women in the courtroom who did.

That next year, I was back in control, navigating single motherhood. Thankfully, I had my new career, Jesse's help, and my church family to support me. I was experiencing more and more of God's tangible presence and transforming power in my life. I was becoming someone new.

Someone sober.

Someone strong.

I continued to excel in my career, quickly becoming the kind of employee the company wanted to invest in for future growth and promotion. At the same time, ministry doors were opening. I started visiting the jail with a minister, helping lead services on the inside. Soon, I went through training to facilitate an Alcohol and Chemical Treatment Series program at Work Release for both men and women.

We gained such favor that inmates were allowed to attend services at our church—and many were baptized. Eventually, the mayor of our city recognized my work and presented me with a certificate for my service in the community. It was a stark contrast to the life I had lived before. I was in awe of the favor and opportunities I was being given.

Do they know who I was?

Do they know what I have done?

How is this even possible?

A New State, Same Struggles

Aaron and I eventually reconciled. He came home and started working as an over-the-road truck driver. His routes took him to Texas where he made new friends. Even though we were still married, he was gone most of the time. I was still doing the daily grind alone working, parenting, and keeping everything afloat.

As our five-year anniversary approached, Aaron invited me to join him on a trip to Texas. He wanted me to meet his friends, see the state, and hopefully catch a vision for relocating. I accepted his invitation. It felt good to get away—just the two of us. We had time to talk and dream about a new start in our lives and marriage.

But when we got back home, the old patterns of behavior were still there. I came to the conclusion that nothing would change and kept repeating, "I am NOT moving to Texas!" Life in Fort Wayne made sense. My support system was there—my church, my job, and my family just two hours away. I wasn't willing to trade that stability for uncertainty. Then, three months later, I found out I was pregnant with our third child.

I really wanted to believe that we could keep our family together and that maybe, Texas could offer a better future. Aaron promised that he would take a local truck driving route and be home with us every night. No more long absences. No more solo parenting.

I started casually looking on my employer's website for job opportunities in the Dallas-Fort Worth area, just to see what was out there. I found an outside sales position—a double-band promotion from my current role. I applied, never expecting what would happen next.

My potential future boss was so eager to hire me. He coached me right down to my shoes. He literally said his boss would notice everything. Then came the interview with the executive leader. I had never experienced anything this high-level before. The interviews went great, and to my shock, I got an offer: a 40% salary increase, plus commission, work-from-home flexibility, and a company car.

I stared at the opportunity in front of me, then at the life I was about to leave behind. And just like that, my words changed.

"I guess we're moving to Texas."

Moving to Texas felt like jumping off a cliff with my eyes closed. We left everything behind, to the point of signing the deed to our house over to a local pastor. Settling into a townhome, the plan was to get familiar with the area before buying a house. Jesse came with us, providing an extra set of hands with the kids.

Although Aaron was supposed to find a local job so he could be home with us, he instead took a team driving route with a friend. I was furious. This move was supposed to be our last shot at fixing what was broken, yet we were already unraveling.

The stress was overwhelming. I was navigating a new state, a demanding career, searching for a church home, and juggling motherhood with my father-in-law's help, while I traveled for work. Aaron was gone more than he was home. But despite the chaos, I wasn't alone. I had God.

As the due date of our third baby approached, I kept the pattern of not finding out the gender ahead of time. Aaron made it home just in time for the birth—something I wasn't sure would happen.

The Echo of Empty Promises

Our sunshine girl was born, bringing light into an otherwise stormy season. After a repeat C-section and a tubal ligation, I stayed in the hospital for a few days. Then, Aaron brought me home, picked up my parents from the airport, and just as quickly, left again for the road.

I kept praying for a miracle to take place, for God to restore what felt broken beyond repair. But there comes a point when the reality of staying becomes more suffocating than the pain of leaving. I reached that breaking point, where every day that passed, in the space between yesterday and tomorrow, I felt myself losing pieces of who I was. Those closest to us, friends and family who had watched our struggle, emphatically urged me to consider divorce. Their words were rooted in love, but even so, the thought of walking away was agonizing.

Four years passed from our initial separation before I finally made the hardest, most heart-wrenching decision of my life. In the end, it was the last fragile thread of sanity I held that whispered quietly, telling me I couldn't stay any longer. I had no choice but to let go. The Mask of the Devoted Wife had cracked long before, but now it shattered completely.

I had given everything only to find myself more alone in marriage than I had ever been on my own. No amount of pretending could hold together what was already undone. I knew one thing for certain: I couldn't keep sacrificing myself on the altar of a love that didn't know how to stay. God was never asking me to die on the altar of someone else's choices. He was inviting me to live.

After the divorce, the shame and guilt sank deep into my bones, heavy and unshakable. I carried the weight of a broken home convinced that I had dragged my children through pain and rejection they never deserved. Those years feel like faded photographs, blurred at the edges by my own exhaustion and desperation to stay afloat. I fought so hard for stability, but it always stayed just out of reach.

My kids were my only reason to keep going. They were the lifeline that pulled me back every time I felt myself begin to lose it. And yet, even then, I felt like I was failing them over and over.

There's a particular ache in hearing your child ask, "When will Daddy be home?" and trying to convince them, and maybe even myself, that "Daddy loves you." Each answer I gave felt like a broken promise, patched together with scraps of hope I barely believed anymore. I told myself I was just getting what I deserved, a kind of punishment for my past. But the worst part was knowing that I couldn't protect them from those choices. I watched helplessly as the fallout of my life became theirs.

I thought I understood what it meant to feel powerless. I didn't. Not until I was comforting my children through the tears I had caused. In those moments, it was all I could do not to drown in pity. I mourned the life I had wanted for them, for me. But mourning couldn't fix it.

The Mask of Numbness

The same month my divorce was finalized, my beloved Nana passed away. The double blow sent me into a depression deeper than anything I'd known. I was constantly exhausted, retreating to my bed whenever possible. Even simple tasks like taking a shower felt overwhelming.

At this point, I wasn't using marijuana or anything else to cope. I simply just wasn't functioning. The Mask of Numbness was my desperate attempt to shield myself from the overwhelming pain of my depression. I went through the motions of daily life, but each step felt like I was dragging myself through a thick haze. I couldn't feel joy, sorrow, or anything.

I was just...gone.

In a moment of desperation, I walked into a medical clinic, hoping to get a prescription for Xanax to calm my nerves. The doctor didn't even look at me long before she said, "You don't need that. What you need is an antidepressant." Then she added, without emotion, "Didn't you see the sign on the door? I don't prescribe narcotics." That moment hit me hard—it was a wake-up call, making me realize that my struggles were far deeper than I had ever acknowledged.

Reflection

What have you mistaken for devotion
that was actually self-abandonment?

The Lie Behind the Mask

"Devotion means staying, no matter what.
Even if it is to my own detriment."

The Truth

Sometimes the bravest thing you can do is let go.

Proverbs 3:5-6 (NKJV)
*Trust in the Lord with all your heart,
And lean not on your own understanding;
In all your ways acknowledge Him,
And He shall direct your paths.*

CHAPTER THIRTEEN

A DIVINE TWO-STEP TO LOVE

"Two broken hearts don't make a whole, but they can choose to heal together."
—Angela Martin

On May 10, 2008, I met a man who would become an unforgettable part of my life—who I now call "King David." I can't help but laugh at God's sense of humor. My kids were often under the care of their Papa Jesse, my ex-husband's father. And it was he who introduced me to David. Just like in the Bible, Jesse's son was named David.

Jesse lived around the corner from me, and because the kids' school was within walking distance, I often stopped by his apartment. Many afternoons, I'd be standing under the covered parking, venting to him about his son's broken promises and lack of visits.

More than once, as we talked, a man would pass by on the sidewalk with a big smile and lock eyes with me. Something about him caught my attention. In between sentences, I'd say a quick "hello." As he walked away, a thought whispered in my spirit: "He's a believer."

That Mother's Day weekend, I treated myself to a facial. Jesse took the kids to the apartment pool. When I returned, he met me at the gate with a grin and said, "Some man over there wants to meet you."

I sighed. "Who?"

He pointed toward a man lounging in a chair on the other side of the pool. I glanced over, expecting to see some guy looking for a sugar momma. But when I saw him, I recognized him immediately. It was the man I'd seen before.

Feeling a strange nudge, I walked over. He introduced himself as David. And the moment I heard his name, something in my spirit whispered, "King David."

We chatted for a few minutes. And to my own surprise, I pulled out a church business card, wrote my first name and number on it, and handed it to him. I wasn't even ready or thinking about dating. I was healing. I was doing just fine on my own. If anyone was going to come into my life, they needed to add something, not drain it.

A Date With Destiny

The next day, David sent a simple but thoughtful Happy Mother's Day text. There was something warm in the way he worded it, and I couldn't help but smile.

A few days later, he called. A week later, he asked me to lunch. I told him to pick me up at Jesse's. I wasn't about to let a stranger know where I lived. When I slid into his truck, I caught the scent of clean cologne and fresh gum. I glanced at his jeans and thought, those fit him well. *Don't stare too long! You're a modest Christian woman now!*

We ate at Chili's and talked about work and our kids. At one point—without even waiting to see if there'd be a second date—I blurted out, "Do you want more children?"

"No," he said.

"Same," I replied. I wasn't able to have more children.

After lunch, we stopped by Target, then took a stroll through a park where horses were nearby. As we stood near the fence admiring one of them, an unfamiliar feeling washed over me. A deep, quiet peace I wasn't used to.

In the weeks that followed, we spent more time together. But I made it clear I was planning to move back to Michigan once school ended. I even considered that maybe God had me meet David so I could introduce him to my single friend, Diana. She lived in the same complex and was actively looking for a husband.

I told them both, arranged a meeting at the pool, and waited for sparks to fly. But as David played in the water with my kids, Diana turned to me and asked, "Are you sure he's not for you?"

I laughed. "No, I'm moving."

But David kept pursuing me. I remember driving home after seeing him at the pool, sitting at a red light, feeling a stirring in my belly.

"God, what is this?"

David knew what this was before I did.

From Poolside to Proposal

David soon began dropping hints that he was sure I was his wife. I couldn't believe how confident he was. Then, on June 10, 2008, he planned a special night. He picked me up and halfway through the evening, he said he forgot something at his apartment.

When we walked in, music was playing—the Bee Gees. The table was set with flowers, dinner waiting, candles flickering.

I stood there, stunned.

After dinner, he dropped to one knee, opened an illuminated ring box, and revealed a heart-shaped solitaire diamond, surrounded by four rows of seven smaller stones.

Looking up, he asked, "Angela, will you marry me?"

I was completely overwhelmed, but somehow the word came out: "Yes."

Our romance was a whirlwind. By July 5, 2008, we were married in my parents' backyard in Michigan, surrounded by family and a handful of friends.

Later, David admitted that he had noticed me a year earlier at the pool with my children. He saw the ring on my finger and knew I was married. The following spring, he spotted me again. This time, without the ring.

Curious, he asked Jesse, "Who's that woman and the kids I always see you with?" Jesse explained that I was his daughter-in-law, but no longer married to his son.

From that day on, David started watching for me. Literally.

Now this part always cracks us up. He confessed to using his rifle scope to get a better look at me from across the lot. I joke that he wasn't just scoping out the neighborhood... he was stalking his future wife! If that's not proof that God has a sense of humor, I don't know what is.

Reflection

Have you ever tried to protect your heart so fiercely that you almost missed the gift God was trying to give you? Sometimes, love doesn't arrive when we feel ready—it arrives to show us what true healing looks like when two surrendered hearts learn to dance to God's rhythm.

The Lie Behind the Mask

"If I've been broken before, I can't trust again.
Love will only lead to more pain."

The Truth

True love isn't the absence of brokenness—it's the presence of redemption. When God writes the love story, He choreographs beauty out of ashes and harmony out of two souls who choose to heal as one.

Matthew 19:5-6 (NIV)
'For this reason a man will leave his father and mother and be united to his wife, and the two will become one flesh' So they are no longer two, but one flesh. Therefore what God has joined together, let no one separate."

CHAPTER FOURTEEN

THE SLOW DANCE OF HOPE

"Hope is the thing with feathers that perches in the soul and sings the tune without the words—and never stops at all."
—Emily Dickinson

Wearing a half-mask felt safer than showing up fully exposed. It let me move forward, sort of, while still hiding the parts of myself I wasn't ready to face. David saw me through the half-mask. Maybe because he was wearing one too. My counselor's words echoed in my mind: "A halfway-healed person will always attract another halfway-healed person."

At the time, I brushed it off. I thought I was healed enough, at least healed compared to who I used to be. But the truth was, I still had open wounds that were masked but not mended. I had learned how to smile and look strong, but I wasn't truly free.

Aaron's name was still so fresh on my mind. I caught myself calling David by it more than once and then quickly apologized. Our first year of marriage was a wild mix of love, chaos, and growing pains. My kids lived with me full-time, while their father—recently remarried—had moved to California, and only visited occasionally. David's teenage daughters lived with their mom. We saw them now and then at sports events, but we weren't a cohesive unit.

Blending our lives wasn't some cute little sitcom. It was a storm! What started out feeling exciting quickly turned into a crash course in navigating broken hearts, and the weight of everything we hadn't yet healed from. The honeymoon phase? Gone before it ever really started.

Instead, we found ourselves wading through the tension of merging families, balancing love and loss, and trying to hold it all together. It was one of the hardest years of my life, the closing of one chapter, and the imperfect beginning of another.

I made a decision to wean myself off the antidepressant medication. It wasn't until years later that I learned the medical and mental health community generally advises staying on antidepressants for at least a year after symptoms improve. But I didn't wait. I mistook momentum for wholeness.

Just before Christmas, we placed an offer on a four-bedroom house with a big yard and a cul-de-sac. The home had only been on the market for 17 days! By New Year's, we were closing the door on our past and opening a new one together.

Baby Fever

By spring, a new desire stirred within me. I wanted another baby! Even though David hesitated, I threw myself into research—looking for doctors who specialized in tubal reversals.

I made the appointment by faith, clinging to the dream that maybe this body still had life to give.

The fertility specialist was kind but blunt. They pulled up images of a "normal" abdomen. They then compared them to the internal battlefield of scar tissue left behind by my two previous C-sections. The doctor gently explained that a tubal reanastomosis might not work and recommended in vitro fertilization (IVF) instead.

We left with more questions than answers. After months of hard conversations, and deep soul-searching, we decided to try the surgery. We began saving money, one hopeful dollar at a time.

THE SLOW DANCE OF HOPE   99

On June 12, 2009, we arrived at the office, my heart pounding with anticipation. As I changed into the hospital gown and lay on the operating table, the bright lights above me blurred while I drifted off to sleep.

The next thing I knew, I was waking up in the recovery room, groggy and disoriented. David's bright face was the first thing I saw, though I could tell he was trying to mask concern.

"Did it work?" I asked.

He didn't have an answer.

When the doctor finally came in, her expression was serious. "Your surgery took longer than expected," she began, "Normally, this procedure takes about an hour. Yours lasted over two. The amount of scar tissue made it far more difficult than usual."

She explained that a second doctor had to assist, and that when they tried to confirm reattachment by flushing blue dye through my tubes, the dye spilled out of my abdomen. They couldn't confirm if the surgery had worked.

Her words should have crushed me, but my heart clung to hope that I might one day be a mother again. My faith burned with expectation. Every time there was an opportunity for prayer at church, my hand shot up first. Like the barren women of Scripture, I cried out for a miracle in my womb.

Miracle Conception

On September 18, 2009, I had a strong feeling that I was pregnant. I drove to the store, with nervous excitement, and grabbed two pregnancy tests. I couldn't wait. I ran to the Wal-Mart restroom and took the first one. When I glanced at the result, my breath caught. Two pink lines appeared in the shape of a cross. I stared at it in utter disbelief. I was pregnant!

I skipped to the baby aisle and picked out a soft, light green bib that read, "I Love Daddy". I pictured how I would tell David.

Back home, David was outside mowing the lawn. I said nothing yet. I took the second test and waited for him to come inside.

When I heard the mower stop, I called him into the kitchen. My youngest daughter, Alysha, just three years old, held the bib in her tiny hands.

"Show it to Daddy, David," I said.

He looked at the bib. "You're pregnant?" he asked.

I handed him the test, my heart racing. He squinted at it then back at me.

"I don't know how to read this."

I turned it upright. "Two lines mean positive."

A pause—then unspeakable joy filled the room. We hugged each other. He went back outside to finish mowing the lawn, while I stayed in the kitchen, caught in the wonder of it all.

From Hope to Heartbreak

A few days later, I returned to the Center for Assisted Reproduction for bloodwork and an ultrasound to confirm the pregnancy.

On September 22, 2009, our joy unraveled. The doctor told us the pregnancy was abnormal. "It's either a miscarriage in progress," she said gently, "or an ectopic pregnancy." After the sonogram, the diagnosis was clear: ectopic pregnancy. Surgery was scheduled the next day.

In the aftermath, I lost the fallopian tube on that side. My chances of getting pregnant again dropped significantly. The doctor didn't offer much hope and even questioned whether my remaining tube was functional.

I was heartbroken.

I cried out to God, "Why would you let me get pregnant, only to take it away?"

The miracle He had allowed me, the miracle to conceive—only to let it die.

May 5, 2010, came and went, the due date for the baby we never got to meet. I still clung to the hope of a miracle. We named her Abigail, meaning "a father's joy." Inside I was torn between my love and trust in God, and the gnawing pain of loss.

Hope Again

On July 22, 2010, we received the joyful news of another positive pregnancy test. Three days later, I went to the doctor for blood work to confirm it was a viable pregnancy. But just as quickly, hope was shaken. While at church, the doctor called. My pregnancy hormones were low and hadn't doubled as expected.

At the end of the service, I approached the altar with tears streaming down my face. The woman leading prayer gently invited me to cup my hands and lift them toward heaven, symbolically placing my baby into God's arms, trusting His will.

I didn't want to accept the doctor's report. I stayed in denial another week, clinging to the hope of a miracle. But when the final blood work came in, my fears were confirmed: I had miscarried.

In the months that followed, disappointment became a monthly reality. I would be a few days late, only to see another negative test. The emotional rollercoaster wore me down. I had survived addiction, loss, and heartbreak before... but this sorrow was different. It came with masks I didn't even know I was still wearing.

And so, without realizing it, I slipped into striving mode.

The next mask I slipped on would reveal just how much of me was still performing, and how much I was finally ready to surrender.

Reflection

What dreams or outcomes have you had to release into God's hands,
even when your heart wasn't ready?

The Lie Behind the Mask

"Hope deferred means God has forgotten me."

The Truth

Delays aren't denials—He's still writing the story,
even when the page feels blank.

Isaiah 40:31 (NIV)
But those who hope in the Lord will renew their strength.
They will soar on wings like eagles;
they will run and not grow weary, they will walk and not be faint.

CHAPTER FIFTEEN

THE MASK OF SUCCESS

"We must be willing to let go of the life we planned so as to have the life that is waiting for us."
—Joseph Campbell

In the haze of disappointment, I chased something that promised momentum. I applied for a position in another division of the Fortune 100 company where I worked—one I technically wasn't qualified for. I didn't have an Electrical Engineering degree, but I had grit. Tenacity had always been my currency. Two months later, the offer came. A bigger paycheck, a larger territory, and a title that screamed success.

This new role required me to travel within a 400-mile radius from home. The potential for advancement, along with commission on top of my base salary, fueled my ambition. I quickly earned the nickname "Pitbull with Lipstick," a label that captured my relentless drive.

What I did for a living quickly began to blur who I was. The title and the chase became my identity, a Success-Driven Mask I wore. The accolades were a refuge, a way to boast while quietly begging for validation. I could focus on the outward accomplishments, masking the inward pain that threatened to surface.

In this world of power and performance, I hid behind the image of a confident, capable woman.

Behind the Mask of Success, I managed to stay sober for three years while we tried to have a baby. But after undergoing tubal reversal surgery, dealing with an ectopic pregnancy, and facing multiple failed attempts to conceive, my hope began to fray.

In February 2012, David and I attended a special evening church service centered around the theme of "Hearing God." During the testimony portion, couple after couple shared stories of miraculous conceptions. When the pastor invited anyone believing for a child to come forward for prayer, David and I stood together. In that moment, a flicker of hope rekindled within us.

Afterward, David turned to me and, with deep emotion, whispered that I was his "precious jewel." His words wrecked me. I melted into a puddle of tears as his words touched my heart in ways it had never been touched before. After that church service, while hope had flickered in that moment, disappointment soon took center stage as we continued to live in the waiting.

Masking Pain with Performance

On the outside, I wore the Success-Driven Mask with pride. I quickly rose to become one of the top salespeople in our division, earning a $39,000 commission in one quarter alone. I was invited into high-powered rooms with executives, including the CEO and Jerry Jones, the owner of the Dallas Cowboys. It seemed like the perfect setup.

Meanwhile, faithful and reliable "Daddy David" stayed home with the kids while I traveled three nights a week to different cities. I hosted late-night dinners with colleagues and clients, where alcohol flowed freely, and conversations often drifted into inappropriate territory. I kept my Christian Woman Mask intact, dodging gestures, and guarding my composure. But the high of success gradually waned.

The heartbreak of infertility took its toll, and depression came with a vengeance. Eventually, I turned back to an old coping method—getting high. David was devastated when he found out. He looked at me with disappointment in his eyes and said, "If I'd known you'd go back to that,

I never would've married you." His words cut deep: "If it weren't for the kids, I'd already be gone."

David had lost all faith and trust in me. I could feel the foundation of our marriage crumbling beneath us. I reached out to the minister from Michigan, the one who married us. We had kept in touch over the years, and I think he always felt a responsibility to check in on us. After all, our pre-marital counseling consisted of a single meal at a Big Boy's restaurant.

On one of those calls, I poured my heart out to him. I confessed the crushing loss of two babies, the hopelessness I felt, and my relapse. He prayed for me, and I followed his counsel. I threw out every bit of marijuana and smashed all the paraphernalia. I wanted to be free. I just didn't know how to stay free.

Surrendering the Dream

By June of 2012, at 38 years old, I had finally come to a place of peace. My journal entries from that season reflect a quiet surrender. I had three healthy children. And while another baby no longer seemed part of our future, I found comfort in believing that the ones we had conceived but never held would be waiting for us in heaven. I had tried, and there would be no regrets.

With that acceptance, the weight of disappointment and stress slowly began to vanish. David and I decided to focus on us. For his birthday in August, we planned a much-needed getaway. No kids, no schedules, just the two of us.

We packed light: a two-person tent, a cooler, swimsuits, and plenty of sunscreen, then hit the road toward the state capital. We felt like teenagers again, playful, and present. After leaving Austin, we took our time heading home, stopping at another state park just because we could. The trip was simple, but it was exactly what we needed. By the time we returned home, our connection felt deeper.

A Miracle in May

On September 20, 2012, a familiar feeling stirred within me. I suspected I was pregnant. The next morning, at 4:30 AM, I took a test. To my utter shock, it was positive. I could hardly believe it, so I waited a few more days and took another. Positive again. A week later, a third test confirmed what my heart was daring to hope for. We had conceived!

Most astonishing of all, we realized this miracle had unfolded just after we had surrendered the dream, during our August getaway. Another August conception. Another May due date. It felt like a divine wink, a reminder that sometimes surrender is what makes room for a miracle.

I had a sonogram at 20 weeks. For the first time in all my pregnancies, I decided to find out the gender. My three children were by my side, each one guessing "boy." The sonographer didn't hesitate. "It's a boy!" she announced, and we all erupted in joy.

Our family was growing to six, two boys and four girls. After all the heartbreak, all the moments I thought I had lost hope, God had written a different ending to our story. On May 22, 2013, our miracle baby, Andrew David, was born. Every time I look at him, I'm reminded: don't stop believing. I will tell this story for as long as I live because miracles still happen.

Through the Heartache

As I sit here now, reflecting on this chapter of my life, I open the pages of an old journal from that time. They're tear-stained and raw, full of desperate prayers, and wavering faith. I poured out everything and every mustard seed of belief that carried me through.

To the women and men who have walked this aching path of infertility, loss, grief, and disappointment, I grieve with you. And I pray that the God who met me in my breaking will meet you too. May your heart be held. May your hope rise again—stronger, steadier, and more rooted than before.

Reflection

What are you carrying so gracefully that no one knows it's crushing you?
What dream have you danced around instead of grieving?

The Lie Behind the Mask

"If I appear strong, I won't be seen as broken or barren."

The Truth

God delights in your vulnerability—
your surrender is the soil for miracles.

2 Corinthians 12:9 (NIV)
But he said to me, "My grace is sufficient for you, for my power is made perfect in weakness." Therefore I will boast all the more gladly about my weaknesses, so that Christ's power may rest on me.

Chapter Sixteen

THE MASQUERADE CONTINUES

"At the end of the performance, the mask falls away, and what remains is the truth."
—Unknown

Despite the joy new life brought, the battle inside me raged on. After my youngest was weaned, I went right back to getting high. I was trapped in a vicious cycle. Every time I found a glimmer of hope, my old patterns would resurface, pulling me back into the pit I longed to escape.

It didn't take long before I was sneaking around and using again. The pull was relentless. When David eventually found out, I lashed out in anger and defiance. "Just deal with it! This is who I am!" Our marriage, the fresh start I'd once dreamed of, was starting to unravel. Things only worked as long as he enabled me, while I escaped mentally through my addiction and physically through my job.

In the summer of 2014, I had mastered the art of appearing to have it all together. I was a Sales Manager for a Fortune 100 company, juggling work, motherhood, and a hidden addiction that was slowly consuming me. On the surface, I seemed unstoppable wearing my Wonder Woman Mask. Beneath the façade, I was unraveling, clinging to substances to numb the chaos within.

With all four of my children home for summer break, I occasionally took one of my two older children on an overnight work trip. On August 13, I set out to Arkansas with my 13-year-old son, Aaron. I had booked my favorite hotel, which featured a room with direct access to the in-ground pool and courtyard.

The drive started like any other, a familiar route east through Texas, into Louisiana, and onward to Arkansas. But in the trunk of my company car was a secret: multiple illegal substances and paraphernalia. My paranoia hummed in the background, made worse by the THC oil I'd already consumed.

Not long after crossing into Louisiana and continuing east, we approached a brightly lit sign that read "Vehicle Inspections Ahead." I tightened my grip on the steering wheel as panic surged through me. My mind raced with worst-case scenarios. My son in the backseat, blissfully unaware.

Stopped by the Cops

Approaching the next exit, I made a desperate decision. I veered off the highway, planning to U-turn and find an alternate route. But as soon as I turned left, my stomach dropped. Multiple law enforcement vehicles, officers, and German Shepherds were stationed in plain sight, detaining and searching cars. Belongings lay strewn across the pavement. I was trapped!

Flashing lights and two officers quickly greeted me as I pulled over. My son sat frozen in the backseat. One officer approached the driver's side and asked me to step out of the car while the other stood watch on the passenger side. The world seemed to close in on me as I unbuckled my seatbelt and climbed out of the vehicle, my legs shaking.

The officer wasted no time. "Ma'am, do you have anything illegal in the vehicle?" he asked. For a moment, I considered lying, but I knew it was futile seeing the dogs at work. I reluctantly admitted to having marijuana and a pipe in my overnight bag. My voice trembled as I directed them to the trunk, where the evidence waited like a ticking time bomb.

They confiscated the contraband and instructed me to stand aside while one officer ran my license and registration. I stood there in my company polo, with its unmistakable monogram, in a company car, on company time. My son was sitting just a few feet away, witnessing everything. I could barely breathe as I prayed under my breath, begging God to intervene.

This couldn't be happening. I was across state lines, with my son, under the influence, and holding illegal substances. My career, my family, my entire life were on the line. This was the kind of moment you see in a movie, where the main character hits rock bottom in the most dramatic way possible. Only this time, I was the main character, and there was no director to yell "Cut!"

The first officer returned and asked again, "Ma'am, do you have anything else in the car?" I reluctantly revealed a prescription pill bottle with capsules of THC oil, known as "Rick Simpson's Oil," and another pill bottle with various prescriptions not prescribed to me, including methylphenidate and pain medication. When asked a third time, "Ma'am, do you have anything else in your car?" I firmly replied, "No."

He walked back to his vehicle while the second officer remained in full view of me and the car. I frantically started asking him what would happen next. He explained to me it was best that I had willingly surrendered the illegal substances, sparing them the hassle of using the drug dogs, which would have obliterated my car.

The first officer returned with a "Summons in Lieu of Arrest" in his hand. My heart pounded as he explained what it meant. I was to appear at the designated place and time but, for now, I was free to go. He handed me the document, and as I signed it, a wave of relief crashed over me. I started yelling, "Thank you, Jesus! THANK YOU, JESUS!!"

To my astonishment, the second officer chimed in. "Thank you, Jesus, is right! You could have been arrested. The company car could have been impounded, and your son taken into Child Protective Custody."

As we resumed our journey east, I kept glancing at Aaron in the rearview mirror. I proudly told him repeatedly, "See, son, you always tell the truth no matter what." I turned this into what I thought was a good teachable moment. He sat in silence.

Hours later, we reached the small town where our hotel was booked. Exhausted and irritable, I pulled into a gas station. The events of the day hadn't hit me fully yet, but one thing gnawed at me: my plans to "relax" that evening were ruined. I had nothing to get high with, and the craving was consuming me.

As I wandered through the store, I spotted a man at the register buying rolling papers. My pulse quickened. I followed him into the parking lot, motivated by the pressure of my addiction. With a polite tone, I approached him. "Hey, can you help me find... something?"

He took one glance at me, a professional businesswoman in an embroidered work polo, and his expression shifted instantly. Without a word, he turned away and walked off, leaving me standing there, humiliated.

The Mirror of Truth

I spent that night angry, replaying the events, and agonizing mentally about not having anything to get high with and physically battling withdrawals! I wasn't thinking about what I had nearly gotten away with or my son being along for the ride for "mother-son time." I was incredibly selfish and consumed with worshipping the idol I had erected.

I didn't know how this would end, but one thing was clear: I couldn't keep living like this. This moment would change everything, one way or another. For the first time, I realized that the road I was on wasn't just taking me to Arkansas; it was leading me straight to rock bottom.

When we returned home, I told my husband, David, what had happened. He was utterly disgusted with me and deeply concerned about the stronghold of my addiction. I took so many risks without considering how my actions affected myself or others. I was a slave, and my master was drugs.

Reflection

What pain did you bury beneath your accomplishments?
What applause drowned out the sound of your soul crying for help?

The Lie Behind the Mask

"If I'm impressive, I'll be accepted."

The Truth

God's healing begins where your hustle ends.

Matthew 11:28-30 (NIV)
"Come to me, all you who are weary and burdened, and I will give you rest. Take my yoke upon you and learn from me, for I am gentle and humble in heart, and you will find rest for your souls. For my yoke is easy and my burden is light."

Scan to awaken your soul and embrace
truth for your healing journey.

ACT III

The Torn Script. Hope Rewrites the Scene.

This act chronicles the courageous journey from wreckage to restoration. It is the story of spiritual breakthroughs, healing of wounds, and rebuilding relationships torn by past hurts. Here, marriage becomes a metaphor for covenant, grace, and redemption. The dance of deliverance begins, and a fragile foundation slowly grows strong. This section is a testament to God's relentless pursuit of wholeness, even in the messiest seasons.

CHAPTER SEVENTEEN

INTERMISSION: THE MASK OF DECEPTION

There's a quiet danger in deception, when it's wrapped in what feels good, even helpful. In our world today, one of the clearest examples of this is the growing normalization and legalization of marijuana.

I want to pause here and speak with compassion and clarity. I'm not here to shame or dismiss anyone who has found real relief through medical marijuana under a physician's care. I've seen how it can ease the pain of chronic illness and support those facing the unimaginable like cancer and severe autoimmune conditions.

I acknowledge those realities, and I honor the journey of anyone who is simply trying to get through each day with less suffering. But I also feel a responsibility to speak to a deeper reality, one that often gets overlooked when comfort becomes the only goal. Not everything that brings relief brings healing. I've learned this firsthand, and it's time we talk about it.

Battling addiction? Let's get real. Marijuana was my drug of choice. I started smoking it at 12 years old, and before long, it owned me. Wake and bake? That was my normal. I stayed high all day, every day, until just before bed.

Sure, alcohol tore my life apart more visibly, especially growing up with an alcoholic father and surviving a horrific drunk driving accident at 16. But weed was the quiet captor. It was my escape, my dopamine hit, my counterfeit comfort. I used it in different seasons, for different reasons. Anytime life hit hard, I lit up.

What was once labeled a "gateway drug" is now paraded in the light, wrapped in the language of recreation, wellness, and even spiritual awakening. But let's call it what it is, a trap in disguise. Just because something is legal doesn't make it right. Just because it's natural doesn't make it safe. Marijuana can quietly open doors to spiritual oppression. What may start as relief can quickly unravel into anxiety, paranoia, confusion, or a dulling of the Holy Spirit's voice. It impairs spiritual discernment, making it harder to recognize truth from deception.

Under the influence, I spent time journaling, claiming a heightened spiritual experience and deep revelation, but actually, marijuana flips the divine order. Instead of the spirit leading the soul under the Holy Spirit, the soul takes over and blurs true discernment. Read that again! And perhaps most dangerously, it can become a counterfeit comforter, subtly replacing the presence and power of the Holy Spirit with a temporary, numbing escape.

This isn't judgment, it's a warning. I'm not condemning people who are hurting and just want to feel okay for five minutes. I've been there! But I also know what it's like to wake up years later wondering where your fire, clarity, and purpose went.

As someone who carries a prophetic voice, I have to say it straight. There's a spirit behind the normalization of marijuana that's numbing a generation and silencing destinies. We're medicating our pain instead of facing it. We're trading breakthroughs for a buzz. And that counterfeit peace? It's robbing people of the real thing. I want to spend the rest of my days cultivating an authentic relationship with the Holy Spirit. I've grieved Him long enough.

Reflection

The Spirit of God doesn't dull your pain; He heals it. He doesn't numb your purpose; He ignites it. Anything we run to before we run to God will eventually run us into bondage.

The Lie Behind the Mask

"This is harmless. It's natural, it helps me relax."
Deception often disguises itself as relief. What begins as a way to take the edge off can quietly become a chain around the soul. The Mask of Deception whispers that sin isn't sin if everyone else is doing it—that peace can be found in smoke instead of Spirit.

The Truth

Not everything that feels good is good for you. The Holy Spirit offers what no substance ever can: peace without fog, healing without escape, and joy that doesn't fade when the high wears off.

1 Corinthians 6:12 (NLT)
"You say, 'I am allowed to do anything'—but not everything is good for you. And even though 'I am allowed to do anything,' I must not become a slave to anything."

CHAPTER EIGHTEEN

A STAGE SET FOR SURRENDER

"We admitted we were powerless over our addictions and compulsive behaviors.

That our lives had become unmanageable."

—Twelve Steps

My recovery journey officially began on November 9, 2014, the day I stopped using marijuana and joined my first Celebrate Recovery Step Study. That study became my lifeline, guiding me step by step through the Eight Principles rooted in the Beatitudes, while incorporating the timeless 12 Steps of AA. The purpose was simple but profound: to find freedom from life's hurts, habits, and hang-ups.

Emotions I had buried deep were finally surfacing. My mom had a way of describing it perfectly: she said my emotions were being "unfrozen." It was messy and overwhelming. Confronting those emotions is like tearing open old wounds, each throb a reminder of past pain. It's excruciating, but there was no escaping it. For the first time in years, I wasn't numbing my pain; I was naming it. And that was a miracle.

In Celebrate Recovery, I found what I'd always longed for—a place to belong where I didn't have to perform. I no longer needed to be the "good girl," the "devoted wife," or the one who had it all together. My group became my accountability partners, my lifeline, and my family. They didn't flinch at my mess—they welcomed me with open arms. That kind of grace was both healing and terrifying. Could I really be this loved, even in my brokenness?

It was during this season of my life that I began to uncover a peace and serenity I had never truly known. The old, dysfunctional patterns I once clung to, those compulsive, addictive behaviors that provided only fleeting escape, began to lose their grip.

This wasn't a quick fix. What took years to build in brokenness would take time to undo. God was not just rescuing me—He was re-forming me. It meant letting go of the unhealthy crutches I'd leaned on and replacing them with something better. I discovered the importance of surrounding myself with the right "people, places, and things." Healing isn't just identifying what's broken; it's about rebuilding. Slowly but surely, those new healthy patterns began to take root. I was learning how to live.

It was my dad's birthday, January 26, 2015—the day I chose to bury my bondage. I didn't just throw away my paraphernalia; I waged war. With every shattered pipe and torn-up stash, I made a prophetic declaration: I am done dancing with demons. This was more than cleanup—it was a symbolic act of deliverance for our entire bloodline. A line drawn in the spirit that said, "This territory is no longer yours." That day, I dismantled an altar.

Healing One Page at a Time

One of the most transformative tools in recovery is journaling or, as some call it, a daily inventory. I wrote like my life depended on it—because in many ways, it did. Pages and pages poured out of me. Grief, rage, confusion, longing. I wrestled with God on the page. I asked hard questions. I didn't censor myself. And in the mess of ink and tears, I began to hear Him speak back—softly at first, then with more clarity. His words became the ink of redemption.

Flipping through those journals now, I'm struck by how much I would've forgotten if I hadn't written it down. On the page, they live on, reminding me how far I've come.

My life felt like an endless war, both with the world and within. I poured so much energy into worrying about things I had no power to change. I tried to escape pain through denial and distraction. I told myself I was fine.

Anger and resentment are heavy chains, and I carried them everywhere I went. They locked me in place, keeping me from freedom and peace. If I didn't rely on anyone, I couldn't be hurt by anyone. If I didn't trust, I couldn't be betrayed. I built walls, thinking I was protecting myself, but those walls also kept love out.

In that isolation, I started to believe lies that whispered, "No one really cares about you. No one sees you. No one understands." Those lies hollowed me out, leaving a deep, aching emptiness. But recovery began to teach me that vulnerability is not weakness. The truth we hide from is often the very thing that can set us free.

The Reckoning in the Reflection

Recovery has a way of stripping away the noise until you're left with just one thing: the person in the mirror. It's uncomfortable—sometimes excruciating—to meet that gaze head-on.

I often asked myself, "Who am I?" Not the version I showed the world, not the person shaped by expectations. But me. The real me. And honestly, I wasn't sure I wanted to know the answer.

Isolation felt safer. I told myself that if people knew the truth—the unedited version of me—they'd walk away. So, I stayed hidden, even while surrounded by people. It was easier to drown myself in distractions: work, mindless busyness, anything that kept my mind too occupied to ask hard questions. Sometimes it was just piling task after task on my shoulders. But no matter what I used to fill the void, the war inside raged on.

I hid behind a thousand masks, juggling a façade of normalcy while living what felt like a double life. The truth was, I was using all day, every day. Every moment of irritability felt like too much. Riding in the car with my family was hard. The kids' laughter and constant chatter pierced through me, grating on my nerves. David's careful driving and tendency to go under the speed limit, infuriated me.

But I couldn't recognize the goodness in any of it. Not the beauty in my children's voices, or the stability my husband tried to offer. I was locked in a cycle of self-destruction, spiraling further away from the life I thought I wanted, and from the people who needed me the most.

Healing, Not Cured

Recovery is a series of steps that often intertwine, sometimes leading me backward before I could move forward. Healing has not been a straight line, and each day brings its own challenges. But in those moments of struggle, I have also found growth, understanding, and grace.

It wasn't until I realized that recovery was not about perfection but progress that I gave myself permission to be human. This journey has never been about erasing my past. It's been about learning to live with it, and to love the person I am becoming despite it. Growth demands that we stay curious about ourselves and committed to learning, even when it's uncomfortable.

Eventually, I realized: you can't outrun yourself. The mirror will always be there, waiting. The music faded, leaving me standing in the aftermath of my own illusions. The mask I had worn for so long, expertly crafted from layers of false smiles and unspoken lies, began to slip.

It had been my shield, my protection from the world that had hurt me and from the person I had become in response. There was a strange comfort in the mask. It had been my armor, and without it, I feared I might be exposed for the mess I had become. The mask that had kept me hidden from my own pain, from the world, was starting to crack.

As the last notes of the music faded into the silence, I realized that the mask was no longer a shield. It was a prison cage.

There Is More to Your Story

It's terrifying to confront the truth, isn't it? To admit the masks, we wear and the facades we've created. Vulnerability feels like standing in the center of a storm naked with no shield. Without honesty—first with ourselves, then with others—we can never truly be free. The walls we think protect us. They're prisons. It takes courage to start tearing them down, one brick at a time.

If you're in those early stages of recovery, expect this clarity to come too. It won't happen overnight, but it will come. And when it does, you'll begin to see just how much power you have over your own life. Your decisions will start to reflect the truth of who you are, not who you were.

It's not easy to take a courageous step toward healing. Many of us find ourselves entangled in the chains of addiction, often rooted in deep-seated childhood abuse and trauma. Growing up in environments marked by addiction, codependency, and emotional unavailability can leave us with suppressed emotions and no clear path to healing.

A Truth to Behold

You don't have to have all the answers today. You don't have to know how it all will end. You do have the power to take the next step, and that is enough. I've learned that recovery is not about perfection, but progress. It's about learning to show up for yourself, even when the road feels dark and uncertain. It's about choosing to keep moving forward, even if it's just one tiny step at a time. It's about realizing that the pain you're enduring today doesn't have to be your story tomorrow.

You are worthy of healing. You are worthy of peace. No matter where you are on your journey, there is always hope for a brighter tomorrow and for the days ahead. You are stronger than you think, and your story, just like mine, is still being written. The best chapters are yet to come. Keep going because you deserve a life of wholeness!

You might feel alone, but you're not. Seeking support from a trusted mentor or a support group can be transformative. Sharing your story and confronting your fears with compassionate guidance can lead to profound breakthroughs and freedom from the burdens you carry.

It's never too late to start this journey. Embrace the possibility that the depth of your past can become the foundation for a brighter future. Reach out, take that first step, and discover the liberating power of facing your truth. Your journey to healing begins with one brave decision. Do it afraid; you're worth it!

Reflection

Have you ever taken the time to write out your thoughts, even when they're messy or painful? If you haven't tried journaling, I encourage you to start. It doesn't need to be perfect or polished. Just honest.

The Lie Behind the Mask

"It's too late for me. I'll never change. My story is already written."

The Truth

It's never too late to begin again. One brave decision can rewrite my story, and the best chapters are still ahead.

2 Corinthians 5:17 (NIV)
Therefore, if anyone is in Christ, the new creation has come:
The old has gone, the new is here!

CHAPTER NINETEEN

THE SCENE OF FORGIVENESS

"T he only way out is through."

—Robert Frost

Just three weeks into sobriety, we packed up the car in Texas and headed to Kentucky for Thanksgiving. It was my 41st birthday, and for the first time in a long time, I felt present. Not numbed out or under the fog of something altering my mind or mood.

I hadn't realized how much life I'd been missing until I started to feel it again. Even in that short window, breakthroughs started to unfold, one after another. But none hit me like the moment that came with my mom, dad, and youngest sister.

There was no plan for it. No scheduled intervention. Just a quiet moment that opened like a door, and somehow, we walked through it. My sister and I began sharing things we'd buried for years. The kind of feelings daughters carry quietly, not sure if the pain is safe to speak out loud.

I led the conversation. We told our dad what it had felt like growing up without the emotional connection we longed for. We talked about the ache of wanting more closeness, more of him.

Even though it was hard and the timing wasn't perfect, he listened. And before heading upstairs, he looked at us through tears and said, "You'll always be my little girls." Then he said something we had waited our entire lives to hear:

"I'm sorry for the mistakes I made. For not being there the way you needed me."

I couldn't hold it in. Years of pain, confusion, and unmet expectations spilled out through tears. But something else poured out too—healing.

Before I could face others, I had to confront something even deeper—forgiveness. Forgiveness is where true healing begins. It doesn't mean condoning what was done to us or excusing the harm we've caused. Forgiveness is about uprooting the bitterness, anger, and resentment that poison us from the inside out. Holding onto those emotions doesn't hurt the offender. It hurts us. It's like drinking poison and expecting someone else to die.

Forgiveness is a supernatural act. It's not something we can white-knuckle or will ourselves into. It's an act of surrender, a decision to let go of the power those wounds have held over us. In choosing to forgive, we aren't saying it was okay. We're declaring that it no longer defines us.

Forgiveness is the gateway to freedom.

Breaking Free from the Script of Regret

Once I began to heal from within, it opened the door to face the people in my life—my husband, my children, my parents, my siblings, my first husband, and even those I had kept at a distance. Making amends and asking for forgiveness isn't just a nice idea; it's required. It's the only way to break the grip of shame, resentment, and regret that keeps us bound.

This part of the journey brought me to the 4th step: "We made a searching and fearless moral inventory of ourselves." And let me tell you, the battle to reach this step was brutal. It forced me to confront not only the pain others had caused me, but also the pain I had caused—knowingly or unknowingly. It was a reckoning with the truth, the kind that leaves no room for excuses or spiritual bypassing.

After years of denial, fear, and inner warfare, I finally sat down and wrote it all out. It wasn't just a list—it was soul surgery. Every memory felt like a fresh wound. But processing the cause and effect of each one was necessary for breakthrough. You cannot heal what you refuse to name.

This step isn't meant to be taken alone. It requires the guidance of a sponsor or counselor—someone further along in their recovery journey—who can speak truth when you want to run and hold space when the grief hits hard.

I had avoided the 4th Step for years because I didn't want to revisit the trauma, the shame, the things I still blamed myself for. But eventually, grace gave me the courage to press through. It forced me to confront traumatic memories I had long repressed. Putting it all into words was exhausting—emotionally, spiritually, physically.

One of the hardest parts was learning how to balance the pain with the good. The weight of regret threatened to eclipse every moment of beauty. But healing demanded a full picture. Not just what was broken, but what had been preserved.

The Spirit's Call to Radical Forgiveness

After overcoming countless internal battles to complete my inventory, I came to the next crucial step, the 5th Step: "We admitted to God, to ourselves, and to another human being the exact nature of our wrongs." In recovery circles, there's a saying: "We are only as sick as our secrets." And I had many.

These hidden parts of my story kept me trapped in the past, preventing me from fully living in the present. Sharing them out loud with someone else is a vital part of the healing journey. This step was challenging, but it led to a significant breakthrough.

I'll never forget the day I walked into the office to meet with my sponsor to talk through what I had finally found the courage to face.

When I reached the memory that had haunted me the longest—the car accident at 16 that left a dear friend paralyzed—I broke.

I felt something deep inside me shatter. It wasn't just tears or words; it felt as if a cord of shame, tightly wound around my soul for decades, snapped! With that release came a surprising gift; a measure of peace I didn't know was possible.

There's something powerful about speaking the truth out loud. Shining a light on the lies robs them of their power. We weren't created to carry these burdens alone. Isolation only feeds the lies that keep us bound, giving our demons permission to linger in the shadows.

After that, I committed fully to the process. My mind cleared. My emotions stabilized. I began seeking forgiveness from those I had hurt, layer by layer, like peeling back an onion. Each conversation revealed more buried pain—but also brought me closer to wholeness.

This was no longer about staying sober. It was about becoming free.

Unveiling the Truth Written on My Soul

The true turning point came when I began to repair my relationship with myself. I had missed so many of my kids' sporting events and family outings—moments I can never get back. Coming to grips with that was difficult.

Sometimes I was too depleted to get ready or too ashamed to face anyone. Other times, I'd pick a fight with David just to create an excuse to stay home, alone with my addiction. I can still see them pulling away in the car while I stepped in the opposite direction, chasing the next high. The shame was suffocating. I hated myself. I was failing at everything that truly mattered.

I wasn't living. I was barely surviving. Frequent panic attacks, overwhelming regret, and the weight of my failures kept me shackled. The transition from bondage to freedom didn't happen all at once. It was slow. Sometimes one breath at a time.

Of all the steps in recovery, forgiving myself was the hardest. I had spent years convinced I deserved the torment—the guilt, the nightmares, the anxiety. I felt unworthy of love and incapable of peace. I ran from anything that might help me, clinging to punishment like it was my penance.

But learning to forgive myself required surrender. It meant laying down the lies I'd believed and trusting that freedom wasn't just for other people—it was for me too. And as hard as that was, it was worth it.

Letting go and forgiving myself felt like cords of darkness being severed. Instead of running from my past, I chose to embrace it. And in that surrender, I found strength. I accepted the things I could not change and the door to peace swung wide open. Today, I walk in gratitude and hope, and I extend that same invitation to you.

This journey isn't easy. It strips away the layers of denial we've hidden behind. It surfaces wounds we thought were healed or convinced ourselves "weren't that bad." But with each tear, with every painful memory faced, those wounds begin to lose their power.

Change only comes when the pain of staying the same outweighs the fear of transformation. That truth has guided me again and again. So, I'll say it plainly:

Embrace the discomfort. Let it lead you. Your freedom is on the other side. And your life—your real life—is waiting to begin.

A Truth to Behold

If you're standing on the edge of this step, I see you. It's terrifying. But freedom is on the other side. Facing the truth, no matter how painful, is the only way to break the chains. Take the step. It will change everything. You don't have to change everything overnight. But today—right now—you have the power to choose. This is your invitation.

Right now, ask yourself: What does your life look like through the lens of your current choices? Are you walking in clarity—or hiding from a memory you've tried to ignore?

Recovery offers you something priceless: the chance to reset. To live from truth instead of trauma. To make choices from a place of stability instead of survival.

Pause. Take a deep breath. Imagine falling asleep in peace. Waking up with joy. Trusting yourself again, not because you've done everything perfectly, but because you know who you are now and no longer define yourself by who you used to be.

Maybe your first step is setting a boundary. Calling a counselor. Saying "no" to something that drains you. Or simply giving yourself permission to feel without judgment. Whatever it is, take it. Your original design and destiny are waiting. You hold the keys. What will you choose?

Reflection

What have you buried in silence,
afraid that speaking it will make it more real?
What would it cost to finally let someone in?

The Lie Behind the Mask

"If I hide it well enough, I won't lose love."

The Truth

The truth won't destroy you—it will set you free.

Psalm 32:3–5 (NLT)
When I refused to confess my sin, my body wasted away, and I groaned all day long... Finally, I confessed all my sins to you and stopped trying to hide my guilt. And you forgave me! All my guilt is gone.

CHAPTER TWENTY

CENTER STAGE: THE REAL ME

"The depth of your past will be the height of your future."
—David Martin

Recovery felt like taking baby steps. It wasn't a sprint, but little by little, life began to improve. You might not see it right away, but change is happening. I promise you that.

I remember reaching the 90-day milestone—monumental in early recovery. Suddenly, I could think clearly again. As my mind cleared, so did my expectations. I stopped demanding perfection from myself and others. I began to trust the quiet wisdom inside me, the voice I had ignored for so long.

You'll realize something powerful on this journey: you are not who you were, and you're not stuck where you started. I wasn't locked in a loop of self-destruction anymore. I didn't need to audition for love or hustle for worth.

That's what insanity does. True sanity—real wholeness—is about living in the light of truth. Not the lies. Not the trauma scripts we once obeyed. The Mask of the "Functional Addict" had to be laid down at the feet of Jesus. That version of me died so the true me could rise.

One of the most vital lessons I learned was this: you can't heal in isolation. I needed people. Friends. Mentors. Accountability. Yes, even when I didn't feel like it. The greatest trauma might not be what happens to us. It may be the belief that we have to go through it alone. That's the lie the enemy loves to feed us in the dark.

For years, I lived under that lie. I wore the Mask of Self-Sufficiency while starving for connection. I thought if anyone saw the real me, they wouldn't love me. But then again... who was the real me?

The mask had been on for so long, I forgot. My career became a costume. It kept me moving fast enough to avoid seeing the pain in my family's eyes. It gave me something to point to, something to prove I was still "successful," even when I was spiritually bankrupt.

I wasn't rushing to rewrite my life overnight. Instead, I was learning to walk in rhythm with God. This was the beginning of an unmasked life—anchored not in performance, but in presence.

From Career to Calling

After more than a decade on the road, my heart longed for home. I wanted to wake up next to my husband, not in another hotel room. My oldest daughter had just started high school, and I refused to be a part-time, passive parent. No more hiding in addiction. No more hiding in work. It was time to be present.

When my annual review came up, I sat across from my sales director and told him my decision: I was coming off the road. No more miles between me and the people who mattered most.

He looked up from his notes and nodded. "I respect that," he said. "Let's find you something else, something that keeps you home."

For the next nine months, I eased into a new reality—working from home while helping train my replacement. I sat in on interviews, made joint trips to key customers, and gradually handed over the reins. My employer offered me two roles in Commercial Operations, both allowing me to stay home.

It should have felt like a win. But deep down, it felt like a compromise, like settling for something safe instead of stepping into what my heart was truly calling me to do. I followed that leading and exited my career the following year in January.

On January 29, 2016, after 12 years and 3 months, I stepped away from the familiar and into the unknown. It was a strange paradox in grieving the loss of what had been while celebrating the victory of moving forward.

Resigning from my career left an open space, and almost immediately, two invitations came to serve on Boards of Directors. The ambition in me said yes to both. My days filled up again, each new responsibility pulling me into uncharted territory.

One of these ministries led me across the world to South Africa on a missionary trip. The experience was nothing short of life-changing, stretching me in ways I hadn't expected and confirming that stepping into the unknown was exactly where I was meant to be.

Transitioning into a full-time stay-at-home wife and mother of four wasn't easy. My identity had been tied to what I did. I could wear my Successful Businesswoman Mask, stay busy to ignore the war inside myself, and recruit David and others to handle the mundane tasks.

This wasn't my first time stepping into the role of a homemaker. I had adored being home during my first marriage, raising my two children. But this time, everything felt different. I was different.

The innocence and joy of that earlier season had long since faded. Years of high stress had conditioned my nervous system to live in hyper-vigilance. The tenderness I once carried had been replaced with a hardened edge and a short fuse.

Leaving my career didn't magically fix any of that. Instead, it dropped me into the middle of an identity crisis. No drugs to numb the pain. No job to distract me. No fat paycheck to validate my worth. Just me and the uncomfortable task of facing who I had been... and who I was becoming.

Undone in the Dance of Intimacy

I spent Friday nights at Mansfield House of Prayer (MHOP) that met at Mansfield Dance Academy. It was unlike anything I had ever experienced. I had been a Christian for 14 years, but I had never learned how to be still with God. I was so used to doing—serving, striving, surviving—that I didn't know how to simply be with Him.

That little house of prayer became my safe place. A sacred space where worship wasn't rushed, where I could sit at His feet without an agenda. For the first time, I felt free to seek God with my whole heart—and not feel ashamed. A stillness met my chaos and soothed it.

It was there I began to hear His voice more clearly. Not audibly, but in the quiet moments of journaling, reflection, and simply learning to listen. The leaders at the House of Prayer gave language to things I had experienced my whole life but never knew how to explain.

Through their guidance and the Holy Spirit, I came to understand the gift of prophecy. My spiritual eyes began to open. I learned to recognize the difference between my voice, God's voice, and the voice of the enemy. God is always speaking, and all His children are wired to tune in and respond.

Life's wounds and trauma can block us from hearing God's voice. During this season, I received a personal word from a minister that anchored me. I'd like to share it with you as the same spirit of prophecy is speaking over your life today:

"The brightness of His glory is shining on you. Rays of light are piercing through the darkness—the blackest darkness—exposing the hidden things of darkness that have been like spider webs trying to hold you down. They are severed in Jesus' name!

My daughter, you need to know that I'm the One who did this. It wasn't something you did; it's something I did. I chose to do it—for liberty, so that you would be set free from your past!"

Behind the Curtain of My Soul

Hearing His voice became my lifeline, drawing me back to my Father and attuning my spirit to the frequency of Heaven.

This part of my story of learning to be still and hear could fill an entire second book, but I just want to leave a simple summary of it here for you, because its effects were profound. This was when I learned what it meant to be led by God, not just in theory, but in the quiet moments of listening and trusting His voice.

You have the same invitation. No matter where you are in your journey, you can learn to be led, too. His voice isn't reserved for the few. He wants to meet you in the stillness. Slow down, be still and behold Him. He will come. And when He does, everything changes. Selah.

Learning to hear God's voice wasn't just a spiritual milestone. It was the start of a holy unraveling. Something awakened in me. I felt an urgency to dive deeper, to discover what it meant to walk in my calling and serve others through spiritual gifts.

One afternoon, in my quest of more of Him, I stumbled across a ministry offering prophetic training. Everything I read resonated deep within me. I spoke to David about my desire to pursue this and applied. It felt like stepping off a cliff with nothing but faith as my parachute.

After a phone interview with a trainer, I was accepted into the Master in Prophetic Ministry program. My heart soared. I was ready, or at least I thought I was.

I jumped, turning in my first lesson with pride and anticipation. But when it was returned, rejected and marked for revision, I was stunned. All my life, I had excelled at writing and expression. I had never been told, "Go back and do it again." My ego took a hit I didn't see coming.

My trainer nicknamed me "Angela Martin 101." While my answers were thorough, they were rooted in head knowledge. Polished and intellectual but disconnected from the raw intimacy God was drawing me into. I didn't realize how much unlearning I needed.

This was no longer just ministry training. It was a stripping away of every identity I had clung to. Titles, talents, and accomplishments. None of it could stand in the fire of what God was doing in me. I wasn't just learning how to minister. I was being undone, and, in the undoing, I found Him.

In the ache of surrender and tears, Jesus met me. Each mask I wore, every wall I built melted like wax in the heat of His love. This wasn't just school. This was heart surgery, and He was healing me from the inside out.

Marked for Destiny

Several weeks later, God orchestrated an encounter that left an incredible mark on my spirit. Encounters like this are rare along my journey; I can still count them on one hand.

It was a Friday night at Mansfield House of Prayer. Guest speaker Riaan De Lange had traveled from Kroonstad, South Africa, and his presence had drawn a crowd. There was a tangible buzz in the room about him being a prophet of God. After worship, he shared a message about John the Baptist, exploring how he was more than a prophet. At the conclusion, he began inviting people forward to minister personally.

David and I stepped up, and he began to prophesy: "I see a great door before you... a new door. A different door. But this time, there is a mutual agreement. Walk through it. You know what it is—it's a business."

He instructed us to hold our hands out before us. "I want to anoint your hands," he said, "that God will give you power to gain wealth." After anointing our hands, he turned to me and said, "Look at me if you can, ma'am. Here is the truth of the business: according to your prayers and your words, he will prosper."

A jolt of power surged through me, but what happened next caught me completely off guard. He walked back, blew over my face, and I felt the Holy Spirit's breath and fire engulf me from the inside out. It catapulted me into another realm of the Spirit. I had to step into the next room to catch my breath and walk off the intensity.

God used this man to mark me that night in a personal and powerful way. I walked away changed—touched deeply, reminded that His power is real, and that when we surrender fully, God moves in ways that surpass our understanding.

As God stripped away the layers of who I thought I was, one truth rose to the surface. My life had always been marked by a battle. From the very beginning, the war had already begun. I was conceived before my parents graduated high school or were married. Before I could walk or talk, the enemy had already tried to derail God's plan for me. The call on my life placed a target on my back.

The enemy heard the announcement over my destiny before I was even born. He came to steal, kill, and destroy, as he always does. The rejection I faced, the pain I carried, wasn't random. It was a relentless attempt to stop me from ever knowing who I truly was. But instead of destroying me, it drove me straight into the arms of Jesus.

I became desperate for the kind of love only He could give. A love that sees the mess and stays. A love that heals and restores. The world had nothing to offer that could fill the emptiness inside me. People let me down time and time again, but God never has. He is faithful.

A Truth to Behold

Maybe your story doesn't look like mine. Maybe you weren't aware of the invisible war over your life, or maybe you've always felt its weight. You might be in the thick of the battle right now, wrestling with rejection, trying to find your identity, or longing to feel seen.

Your pain is not wasted. The ache you feel deep in your chest, that longing for something real, is the place where God loves to meet us. Not when we have it all together, but when the mask melts and falls away, and we finally say, "I can't do this alone."

The same God who pursued me when I didn't know who I was, who gently peeled back my defenses and healed the broken places, is pursuing you too. It doesn't matter whether you're full of faith or full of questions. He's after your heart.

I encourage you to give Him access today. He's standing at the door of your heart, ready to be invited in. He'll rush in with the kind of love that changes everything.

Lay down the mask. Step into the light.
He's been waiting for you all along.

--- ◆ ---

Reflection

What part of your identity have you
hidden behind performance or success?
What would it feel like to be fully seen and still loved?

The Lie Behind the Mask

"If I keep it together, no one will see how broken I really am."

The Truth

God's love doesn't require perfection—only surrender.

Ephesians 2:8-10 (NIV)
For it is by grace you have been saved, through faith—and this is not from
yourselves, it is the gift of God— not by works, so that no one can boast. For
we are God's handiwork, created in Christ Jesus to do good works, which
God prepared in advance for us to do.

CHAPTER TWENTY-ONE

THE MIDNIGHT MASQUERADE

"Sometimes the only way to see yourself clearly is to watch everything fall apart."

—Unknown

With a year of recovery and fresh ministry experience behind me, I stepped into the new year with a hunger for deeper clarity. I committed to a 40-day fast, silencing the noise to hear from God.

One morning, I felt drawn to a book that had been untouched on my shelf for years—a gift from my cousin, *The Purpose Driven Life* by Rick Warren. I dusted it off and began reading one chapter each day. I didn't skim. I journaled, reflected, and let the truth of each chapter sink in.

Those 40 days became some of the most intentional and transformative mornings of my life! I wasn't just fasting from food. I was fasting from confusion, striving, and the need for outside validation. I wanted direction. I needed clarity.

Even though I had taken a 180-degree turn by leaving my six-figure career, I still had to confront where I was finding my worth. Ministry, I realized, can be just as addictive as a career if you use it to replace your identity.

After years of misplaced priorities, I had to face the truth. I needed to give my first attention to the people entrusted to me—my husband, my children, and my own soul.

We can easily exchange one kind of busy for another. We can chase applause, achievement, or acceptance, even when it's dressed up in spiritual language.

During that time of stillness and seeking, I asked hard questions: Who am I, really? Why am I here? Slowly, answers began to form, truths that would later anchor me through seasons of rejection and closed doors, and steady me when new opportunities came rushing in.

Toward the end of that 40-day journey, I sensed a strong pull toward something David and I had talked about for years. Building something together to combine his passion for fitness with my passion for freedom. We named it Super Natural Life. At first, I didn't know if it was meant to be a ministry or a business. I kept asking God.

Then one morning, in quiet prayer, I heard words so clear they might as well have been audible:

"Your business is your ministry."

Those five words changed everything. It would take years to unpack the depth of what God intended to do, but I knew this: it wasn't about choosing between profit or purpose. It was about building something rooted in both.

This is a signpost for you, too. Maybe it's time to ask yourself the same questions. Take time to seek. Not to perform, but to uncover the purpose you were designed for. It's not about chasing significance but stepping into alignment with the life you were made to live.

Behind the Mask of Panic

As I neared the end of my two-year prophetic ministry training, I came under direct spiritual attack from the spirit of fear. It wasn't subtle. It was targeted and relentless.

During this season, I became convinced that fear had been a generational stronghold in my family—running through patterns of anxiety and hesitation to step fully into purpose. I could trace it back two generations. Its grip was undeniable.

As I began to rise up in recovery, business and ministry, the enemy came for me with a vengeance.

The battle almost always came at night. I would settle into bed, trying to rest, but my thoughts would spiral into dark corners of what ifs, worst-case scenarios, and irrational but convincing fears.

Then the physical symptoms would hit. My heart pounding, breath shortening, a cold rush of dread surging through my body like electricity.

I'd get up, splash cold water on my face, breathe deeply, and pray for it to stop. But moving almost made it worse. There was nowhere I could go to escape it. The darkness felt impenetrable. It fed my panic even more. The first few times it happened, I thought I was having a heart attack.

When these attacks became frequent, David told me to wake him so he could pray with me. That brought relief. Sometimes I would even step outside in the middle of the night, look at the moon, hoping it would break the grip.

There were nights I swore I heard bugs crawling on the floor and walls. I'd jump out of bed, turn on the lights, and grab the bug spray from the laundry room, but nothing was there.

At first, I thought maybe it was stress. But the episodes kept coming. The sensations were too real. I couldn't ignore them.

Desperately confessing Scripture out loud helped push back the darkness. These attacks weren't entirely unfamiliar. I remembered similar panic when I was high years ago. The clinical term may have been panic attacks, but I knew there was a deeper reality. This was spiritual warfare.

This was torment. Not from flesh and blood, but from principalities. This wasn't random. It was strategic, designed to make me feel powerless and unstable.

Fear doesn't just paralyze you; it distorts reality. It convinces you you've lost control. Fear had been the stronghold, but God was ripping off its mask and revealing it for what it truly was. I was no longer willing to give it ground.

These attacks continued for over a year. As I brought these experiences to prayer, something began to shift. God started unmasking the fear. I realized the enemy wasn't attacking me because I was weak, but because I was becoming dangerous. He wanted to shake my mind because he feared my calling.

When you begin to take ground in your God-given purpose, the enemy doesn't sit back quietly. He responds with intimidation, distraction, and confusion, hoping you'll retreat before you realize how powerful your obedience really is.

Fear was his last-ditch effort to derail me. The panic and torment weren't just symptoms; they were signals. Signals that I was stepping into territory hell didn't want me to claim.

A Truth to Behold

If you find yourself in a similar battle, don't shrink back. Don't surrender your momentum. You will overcome because the One who called you is faithful, and His power is greater than anything that comes against you.

Reflection

Where has fear disguised itself as control in your life?
What would it look like to live unafraid, fully trusting God?

The Lie Behind the Mask

"If I can control every outcome, I will feel safe."

The Truth

Perfect love casts out fear—and His love never fails.

II Timothy 1:7 (NKJV)
For God has not given us a spirit of fear,
but of power and of love and of a sound mind.

CHAPTER TWENTY-TWO

TANGO WITH THE GRIP OF GRIEF

"What we once enjoyed and deeply loved we can never lose, for all that we love deeply becomes a part of us."
—Helen Keller

December 20, 2018, a day that shattered the rhythm of our lives, leaving nothing untouched. It wasn't just an interruption; it was a collision. A before and after that redefined everything.

It was a regular Thursday morning. The first thing I noticed when I woke up was that an unknown woman had blown up my Messenger app inbox with frantic messages. She pleaded for me to get a hold of her immediately. My first thought was, "I've never met this woman before. Does she want to ask me for money?"

It was the last day of the semester before Christmas break, and I had my hands full. I dropped off our youngest son, Andrew, at elementary school, and our youngest daughter was home sick. My husband hadn't left for work yet, as he was going in late in order to attend Andrew's school winter party.

Then, at 8:01 a.m., I received a heart-stopping message from a second woman. It was from the ex-wife of my first husband, Aaron. She wrote that a woman was trying to reach his family because Aaron was found dead in his truck.

I couldn't breathe.

The words coiled around me like a boa constrictor. I ran to our bedroom and woke David, hysterical, struggling to get the words out. I told him what I had just heard, but I didn't want to believe it. It didn't feel real.

I messaged the unknown woman back, asking for her phone number. I needed to hear the truth, but even as I dialed her number, I hoped somehow, it was a different man found dead. When she answered, the truth sideswiped me like a speeding truck, leaving me stunned and in shock. I could barely grasp it, but I listened as she told me the details the authorities had given her. Aaron was gone.

He had mentioned some health issues, but I never asked if he was seeing a doctor. For years, I carried the weight of guilt for not doing so. I wondered if things could have been different had I just asked. I didn't tell him I loved him, and I regretted it in that moment. I stayed silent, caught between the boundary of respect for David and my own heart.

The truth was, I loved him—always had, always would. Even though I never said the words, I know he knew. Not saying them still pursues me.

Pain Too Deep for Words

The next moments were agony. My head was pounding. It felt like I had been beaten in the head by a lead pipe. I had to break the news to my children, one by one.

First, I went upstairs to our oldest daughter, Ashlee's room. She was living at home, attending her first semester of college. She was still asleep, and I laid down beside her. She stirred and asked me what was wrong.

The moment the words left my mouth, she started weeping uncontrollably. My heart shattered as I held her tight, praying to God for comfort, for relief from this unbearable pain. I wanted to make it stop, to wake up from what felt like a nightmare, but there was no escape.

Our youngest daughter was home sick from middle school, resting in her bed. I walked into her room, and without me saying a word, she looked up and said, "I don't want to know."

Our oldest son, Aaron II, "Ronny," was a senior in high school, taking his semester exams. I decided not to pull him out early, hoping he wouldn't hear the news through social media. Instead, I sent him a text, urging him to come home right after school.

He got a ride with his best friend to his house, and I went by to pick him up. As we were heading home, I told him I needed to talk to him before he left again with friends. When we arrived, I went upstairs to his room and I began by telling him we might need to take a trip up north soon. He asked, "For what?" He could sense that something awful had happened.

He was in his closet looking for something to wear, and he asked, "Is it my dad?" I could barely speak, but I managed to say, "Yes." Then he asked, "Is he dead?" I whispered, "Yes."

My son, the one who had always been so strong, ran downstairs and collapsed in the hallway. He shook and wailed—a sound so gut-wrenching it tore through me. I screamed in agony and collapsed on top of him, holding him as tightly as I could. Ashlee was right there; her arms wrapped around us both. After a moment, he pulled away, went upstairs, and changed his clothes. He wanted to leave. I let him go. In that moment, I knew that nothing would ever be the same again.

Questions Heaven Has Yet to Answer

As I type this, I feel nauseous. The broken hearts remain; my children's shattered dreams still echo in the corners of their lives. A part of all of us died that day with Aaron. The questions linger, unanswered, as I search for understanding of why this happened. I had finally achieved the best of both worlds.

I had been married to David for 10 years. Longer than the eight years I was married to Aaron. I had worked hard in my recovery over the past four years, and the healing and forgiveness it brought allowed me to rebuild a relationship with the father of my three beautiful children.

The last time I saw him, less than a month before he passed, he was visiting us at our home in Texas with David and the kids. I was getting ready to leave for my evening Zumba class, and Aaron stayed behind to visit.

That moment, that peace we had found, was a supernatural restoration I never thought possible. We had finally reached a place in our lives where the past was healed. We had come to terms with everything. And then, just like that, he was gone.

"Why did God let this happen?" I asked myself this question time and time again. My heart was aching with a grief that felt like it would swallow me whole. I had worked so hard to rebuild our lives. I had fought for healing, for restoration, and now this? Was it all for nothing? We had plans.

I thought we had decades left together. I imagined him walking our daughters down the aisle, laughing with his grandchildren, sharing in the milestones of their lives. And now, all of that was ripped away, leaving me in this unthinkable void. How could this be real? How could he be gone?

My dad was the first to come. As soon as he heard Aaron died, he jumped in his truck and drove through the night from Michigan to Texas. When he walked through our door, I collapsed in his arms.

A few days later, my mom and others followed, just in time for Christmas. They helped us navigate those first hollow, surreal days of grief.

That Christmas changed everything. Even now, Christmas carries a different feeling. It took years. But somehow, Aaron is even more present now than he was in the chaos of our loss. His last Facebook post read, "Merry Christmas to you," with a YouTube video attached of Nat King Cole's - "The Christmas Song" (1961)

Aaron's mom handled the funeral details near her home in the South Side of Chicago, choosing to wait until after New Year's Day. I was wrecked. Breathing felt like a task, moving in slow motion.

David—God bless him—drove us all to Chicago. He was our anchor, a quiet kind of strength that held us together, watching as his wife unraveled with grief over her first husband. With God's help, he gave me room to mourn; he honored my love for Aaron. He never made me feel like I had to choose. Love that deep doesn't disappear just because life moves on.

We were all there for the memorial service and lined up in the funeral procession. Ashlee, Aaron, and Alysha walked just behind Aaron's mom and his brother, who led the procession. David, Andrew, and I were next. Behind us came Aaron's two sisters and their families. I include these details because they matter. We were part of Aaron's story to the very end.

The service was a blur, like a dream you can't wake up from. The songs looped like a heartbeat, and one gospel song, "Praise is What I Do," was etched in my heart. For years after, I couldn't hear it without crying. Even now, it hits differently.

Near the end of the service, the minister invited anyone who wanted to speak. Two cousins I didn't recognize came up—did a kind of spoken word-meets-Rastafarian tribute, complete with bongos. It was heartfelt, but I felt something stirring in me. Aaron deserved words about his life, about what he meant, about how deeply he impacted those around him. The invitation came again, one last call, and I knew. I had to go up. Led by the Holy Spirit, I walked to the front.

I honored him. Honored the legacy of a man I had once loved with everything in me. We'd spent the last three years finding forgiveness and healing, and I needed to say it out loud. Not just for the room—but for my soul. For my children. For the memory of what was good and true, and real.

I started with the only words that felt right: "Before Jesus, Aaron was the best thing that ever happened to me."

Everyone who knew our story knew that was the truth. Getting pregnant with him saved my life. He was the reason we moved to Fort Wayne, where I met Jesus. And he was the reason we eventually moved to Texas—where I met David, the man who now stands beside me. Only God can write a story like that. A story that breaks you and still leads you somewhere holy.

During that season, the only words I could whisper in prayer: "I trust You, Lord." Some days, I wasn't sure I meant them, but I said them anyway. Over and over.

God knows the end from the beginning. His plans are still good, plans to prosper us, to give us hope and a future. Hope that reaches past the grave is the anchor that keeps me steady. And I believe, with every fiber of my being, that we will see Aaron again.

Relapse

Grief gripped me in a way I wasn't prepared for. It clouded my mind, weighed down my body, and slowly strangled my will to function. Depression hit me like a tidal wave. Chronic heaviness, hopelessness, and fatigue wrapped around me like a weighted blanket. My children would look me in the eye and say, "You don't seem happy." They were right. They were processing their grief better than I was.

I stopped going to Celebrate Recovery meetings. I didn't call my sponsor. I pulled back from my accountability partners. I isolated, only leaving the house for groceries, the occasional church service, or Friday Night Prayer. I felt like the walking dead.

One day, in desperation, I remembered a leftover piece of a blunt tucked under the patio rug—something a family member had left behind. I grabbed a lighter, lit it, and took a hit, choking on the smoke. I wanted to feel better. I convinced myself it was medicinal, a way to cope.

It wasn't long before I bought my own supply. I didn't hide it from David. At the time, he thought it was helping me. I knew it wasn't relief. It was bondage. As a former addict, I knew the truth about the drug and more importantly, about myself. I've never been someone who could smoke "just a little." When I have marijuana, I smoke all day. It's never manageable.

Ever since I first picked up drugs at the age of 12, I struggled with the inability to maintain my sobriety. I had been clean for four and a half years, my longest stretch yet. Relapse doesn't happen out of nowhere. It's a slow drift—one thought, one compromise, one day at a time.

For me, it started with emotional exhaustion and isolation. Then the mental rehearsing began—imagining escape, entertaining old cravings. I didn't slip into relapse; I walked toward it when I could have turned back. Owning that truth was painful, but necessary to break free from the lie that it "just happened."

The clinical world defines it as a return to substance use after a period of abstinence. But if you've lived it, you know it goes deeper than that. I had built new habits, found support, and experienced freedom, but I wasn't prepared to process this grief. This loss exposed every crack I thought was sealed. Yet relapse didn't take me all the way back to the beginning. It became something else—an invitation to deeper healing.

Joy Comes in the Mourning

I didn't confess the relapse to my sponsor until years later. I stayed in active use until November of that first year following Aaron's death. Deep down, I knew it wasn't a place I could live in, not without forfeiting something sacred.

The enemy was using my grief to pile on guilt, shame, and condemnation. And I couldn't afford to let those roots grow deeper.

Relapse has a way of shaking every foundation you thought was secure. As I continued navigating the painful aftermath of my relapse and the unrelenting grief, journaling continued to be a tool that helped me process my emotions. It was in those quiet, desperate moments of writing that I found glimmers of clarity, hope, and connection to God.

In the brokenness, I found God in a way I never had before. He alone was the One who was there to gather the shattered pieces of my heart. Not in my strength, not on my terms, but in His perfect timing. The Holy Spirit doesn't force us. And this time, I was ready and willing.

It was one of those days in November 2019, when the light broke through. I stepped outside to let the sun soak into my skin. After everything, this small act lifted my spirit.

That day, I made a choice. I chose joy. I chose to believe that God was still building something beautiful. I believed He was taking me deeper into His presence, and higher into the purpose He'd placed on my life.

It hadn't been easy as I recorded more bad days than good. Still, there was a quiet determination growing in me. I looked up to the heavens, past the pain, and fixed my eyes on the One who had never let go of me. I prayed that my spirit would remain tethered to His. That even when my thoughts wavered, my heart would feast on His faithfulness.

Then something began to shift. I had a series of three dreams. Each one pulled back the curtain on old wounds, hurts that hadn't yet healed. In the final dream, I was at a women's conference. The speaker asked a few leaders to pray for me. They laid hands on me, acknowledged my pain, and I woke up in tears knowing God had touched something deep inside me. Healing had begun.

Even now, as I sit down to write, it's December 19, 2024. Six years later, almost to the day of Aaron's passing. I've purposely waited for this day to write this chapter to revisit it, to give it the weight and space it deserves.

I hold my journal in my hands, the words from that time staring back at me. They are raw, unfiltered, and full of the ache I felt as I lived through it. Reading them now feels like stepping back into a season I barely survived.

I'm grateful. Grateful that I wrote it all down—every thought, every emotion, every detail. Grateful that my past self had the courage to capture the trauma so that my present self could try to make sense of it. This chapter isn't just a retelling. It's a reckoning.

Aaron's cause of death was acute respiratory failure. I think he died of a broken heart. He was an over-the-road truck driver, living on his truck, unmarried, isolated. In a way, my children lost their father twice—once to divorce, and now, to death.

There was so much I was mourning, more than just Aaron's death. I was grieving the loss of his future in our children's lives. The death of shared milestones. The presence of a man who had loved them and loved me, even after we separated. We had made peace. He would come to visit. Sit in our living room. Talk with David. Andrew, just a little guy at the time, would hop into his truck and call him "Big Aaron."

I had to surrender my logic and trust God's sovereignty. I had to believe that deep healing was possible. Joy isn't fragile. It's fierce. It's a sign that the enemy didn't win, that the pain didn't destroy you, and that freedom is real and possible. And I'm living proof of that.

A Truth to Behold

You may have faced a kind of loss that feels too heavy to carry. Maybe it's the devastating loss of someone you loved deeply. It could be a loss of a spouse, the premature death of a child, or the heartbreak of your children following the path of your mistakes.

I get it—the way grief can make every day feel like an uphill battle. The plans you once had seem so distant, so out of reach. You look at your life now and wonder how everything changed so suddenly, and why it had to happen.

Loss isn't something that can be easily explained or fixed. I've searched and there's no quick fix that turns pain into peace. It may not feel like it right now, but over time, you can learn to walk again. It won't be easy. It won't be linear. Hope will arrive. Healing will come. In that healing, you'll find strength you never thought you had.

Grief is a process. God heals the brokenhearted.

He did it for me and He can do it for you.

From My Heart to Yours

If you're in a place right now where life feels overwhelming, where grief has settled in, or relapse has left you feeling ashamed or distant from God, I pray you find hope today. God never let go of me. Not once.

God's love for you is constant. And I believe, with everything in me, that He's leading you somewhere deeper—into healing, into peace, into freedom. Just keep holding on, even if it's by a thread. You are not forgotten, and this is not the end.

Reflection

What pain have you tried to numb instead of grieving?
What would happen if you let God meet you in the middle of it?

The Lie Behind the Mask

"If I stay strong and numb the pain, I won't fall apart."

The Truth

Healing begins when you stop hiding and let
God hold the broken pieces.

Isaiah 61:1-4 (NKJV)
"The Spirit of the Lord God is upon Me, Because the Lord has anointed Me To preach good tidings to the poor; He has sent Me to heal the brokenhearted, To proclaim liberty to the captives, And the opening of the prison to those who are bound; To proclaim the acceptable year of the Lord , And the day of vengeance of our God; To comfort all who mourn, To console those who mourn in Zion, To give them beauty for ashes, The oil of joy for mourning, The garment of praise for the spirit of heaviness; That they may be called trees of righteousness, The planting of the Lord , that He may be glorified." And they shall rebuild the old ruins, They shall raise up the former desolations, And they shall repair the ruined cities, The desolations of many generations.

CHAPTER TWENTY-THREE

DANCING IN THE DARK

"In the midst of chaos, there is also opportunity."

—Sun Tzu

As 2020 unfolded, life as we knew it changed overnight. The COVID-19 pandemic swept across the globe, halting routines, closing doors, and isolating millions. The stillness of lockdown stripped away the distractions and brought every struggle, every unresolved emotion, into sharp focus. The world outside and inside felt like chaos.

Our family's challenges during that season went far beyond a global virus. While the world was locked down, my own world was unraveling. Our 13-year-old daughter, Alysha, was silently fighting for her life.

She had just started high school, but instead of walking hallways with friends, she was stuck in her bedroom, attending classes alone on a screen.

At first, I thought she was simply adjusting, but little by little, we noticed changes. She was withdrawing, losing interest in the things she once loved. Something was wrong.

A friend from Celebrate Recovery recommended a counselor. It had been a year since she lost her dad. Grief was compounded by the isolation of starting high school during a pandemic. I knew it was time to get professional help.

I wasn't in a good place either. I was still raw from my relapse and my own grief. We were both drowning but didn't know how to say it out loud.

When the Cry Becomes a Shout

I was in uncharted territory and had trouble navigating these waters. I argued with her counselor, second-guessed their recommendations. I drove her to inpatient evaluations, only to turn around in the parking lot when I didn't feel peace. Her counselor, as required by law, reported a concern for her safety.

Then came the moment everything tilted on its axis. My daughter's silent cry turned into a shout for help. It was the answer to my desperate prayers... though it looked nothing like what I'd imagined. One moment I was quietly eating dinner, the next, I was yelling for David to come help. He stayed calm as he drove us to the emergency room.

Because of lockdown restrictions, only one parent was allowed inside. The moment I stepped through those hospital doors alone, a wave of dread slammed into me like a freight train.

My heart was racing. My hands were trembling. I was trying to stay calm for her, but inside I was screaming. There's no manual for moments like that. No guidebook for what to do when your child is in crisis.

It all happened so fast. Once her situation became clear and stable, the authorities stepped in. I watched as my daughter was escorted in a wheelchair to another part of the hospital, through a separate elevator, with a police officer at her side.

I wasn't allowed to follow. The waiting room was silent and cold. No receptionist. No magazines. Just me, sitting alone in a mother's worst nightmare, texting David while he sat parked in the parking garage. He remained present, keeping the car warm for us, almost as if in protective expectation—rooted in hope.

I did the only thing I knew to do, I prayed. I pleaded with God to surround her with His peace, to cover her with His angels, to hold her where I couldn't.

Hours later, a doctor emerged with questions about her medical history and mine. They told me that she'd be staying overnight, but I couldn't see her or even say goodbye. I felt helpless, as if I had failed to protect her.

Her struggles consumed our family, stretching me to my breaking point. For more than two and a half years, her crisis demanded everything I had and more. But by the grace of God, the destruction stopped.

Alysha faced her healing journey with a kind of grit and grace that brought me to my knees. She agreed to take medication. She opened up in counseling. She showed up for herself, even when it was hard.

One moment I'll never forget: during a school counselor check-in, they asked her, "Are you okay?" She didn't pretend. She didn't mask. She simply said, "No. But I'm working on it."

That's courage.

I couldn't help but notice how her journey mirrored my own. Her symptoms and patterns of behavior resonated deeply with my adolescent years.

I also began to see how my reactions to her pain reflected my father's responses to mine. That realization was both painful and holy. It invited healing in places I didn't know were still broken.

When I had my first daughter, her birth pushed me to confront my addiction. And now, with my second daughter, at the same age when my own battles began, I was being called to face something just as heavy—mental illness.

The unraveling made space for rebuilding. In our brokenness, we found new language for our struggle. Our conversations shifted from anger and resentment to compassion and understanding. We found something beautiful. The kind of hope that doesn't come from avoiding pain, but from walking through it together.

Her Brave Yes

Walking with my daughter through grief and recovery awakened something in me I didn't expect. Her courage pulled me forward. I followed close behind, desperate to understand the world we had both been thrust into.

I dove headfirst into the world of mental health medication, determined to learn everything—every pill, every side effect, every reason behind the prescription.

Anyone who's walked this road knows it's not a straight path. It's a wearying journey of trial and error. What works for one person fails for another. Doses must be adjusted, combinations tested. There are no guarantees, only hope and persistence.

Every trip to the pharmacy became another opportunity for revelation. I stood at the consultation window like a student, asking questions, scribbling notes. At first, I was doing it all for her. But one day, the learning turned inward.

It was during one of those visits that the conversation with the pharmacist hit differently. As he explained how the medication interacted in the brain, I felt a jolt in my spirit. I suddenly had language for what my own mind had been silently battling. Without realizing it, I wasn't just advocating for my daughter. I was tracing the map to my own healing.

I left the pharmacy that day with a new resolve and called my nurse practitioner. I named the medication outright and asked to try it for myself. Starting that medication was a leap of faith. The first couple of weeks were uncomfortable as my body adjusted.

But then... something broke open.

I felt mentally and physically motivated. I wasn't sleeping my life away anymore. I was getting out of bed. Tasks that once felt crushing became manageable. Conversations didn't drain me. I could see hope again.

About nine months in, it felt like I slammed headfirst into a brick wall. The irritability came roaring back, fierce and familiar. My jaw ached from constant clenching. My mind felt thick and heavy, like trying to think through quicksand.

At night I stared at the ceiling, asking God the kind of questions that only come when your heart is breaking in the dark: "Was that healing real? Will I ever be free? Whole for real?"

If you've ever ridden the rollercoaster of mental health treatment, you know this pain. The surge of hope when something finally starts to work—and the crushing devastation when the breakthrough fades. You go from believing again to barely holding on. But here's what I've learned: that wall wasn't the end. It was an invitation.

That wall forced me to ask different questions, to dig deeper than symptom relief. Sometimes healing doesn't stall because you've failed. Sometimes it pauses because Heaven is asking you to uncover the root.

For those who feel like they're hitting a dead end—who feel ashamed for needing to revisit treatment or adjust medication again—hear this: You are not failing. You are fighting. God is still moving.

Hope doesn't expire. Even when it feels hopeless, it still holds. Every step forward is still a victory. Every breath you choose to keep breathing is a testimony.

This is not where the story ends. This is where it deepens. And trust me—glory is still coming.

By April 2022, I sensed God was preparing me for something deeper. I had walked through recovery, forgiveness, and healing, but there were still hidden places in my soul that needed to be set free. That's when I found myself at a birthing center to experience a spiritual birth I didn't even know I needed.

I thought I was there to learn about my blood, but Heaven had other plans. As the morphologist examined my cells, she began to pray. Before I knew it, the Holy Spirit was moving powerfully in that room, exposing and uprooting things I didn't even realize were still lingering. She prayed about, "severe suffering of the soul," and in Jesus' name commanded trauma, soul bondage, and torment to leave me. And it did!

Deliverance came, not in a church, but in a birthing center—a prophetic sign that something new was being born inside of me.

A Plan for Hope

As my daughter began her recovery, we discovered an unexpected anchor in her Psychiatric Nurse Practitioner, Mr. Kimuyu. Even over Zoom during the pandemic, his steady guidance and wisdom helped fine-tune her medications and bring her symptoms under control. Each meeting reinforced my gratitude, and I started calling him our family hero.

When restrictions lifted, and in-person visits resumed, I made a decision that changed my life. I booked an appointment for myself. It was a pivotal moment, one that marked the start of a new chapter in my journey toward understanding and healing.

The day I walked into his office, I was on edge, desperate for something to make it stop. I couldn't sit still, my mind spinning as wildly as my body. Then my eyes landed on a thick, multi-page booklet sitting on the table. Flipping through it, I found a chart comparing depressive disorder to bipolar II disorder. My eyes grew big. Every line felt like it had been written for me. I saw my life—the chaos, the cycles—mapped out in black and white.

When I finally sat across from him, I shook his hand, gratitude overflowing as I thanked him, again and again, for what he had done for my daughter. He smiled and said simply, "You're welcome." Then he asked, "What brings you in today?"

I took a deep breath and let the dam break. I began to open up to him, sharing decades of pain and confusion. For almost two hours, I poured my heart out, each word laden with years of unresolved emotions. As he paused between my words to type notes into his keyboard, I realized just how much I had kept locked away for so long.

When I finished, he leaned forward and said something I will never forget:

"It's a miracle you've survived what you have." Those words didn't feel like pity. They felt like truth. Like freedom.

Everything I had been struggling to comprehend about myself, and my journey began to fall into place. It wasn't just a diagnosis; it was another turning point in my life, one of the most powerful break-throughs of my story.

For years, I wore the Mask of "Proud Survivor." I thought admitting I needed medication or professional help meant I lacked faith—that somehow, if I just prayed harder, worshiped louder, or fasted longer, I could will myself into healing.

But that belief was a lie. It kept me stuck, hiding behind a façade of spiritual strength while silently unraveling inside. God was never asking me to pretend I didn't need help; He was asking me to trust Him enough to receive it. I realized that taking medication didn't diminish my faith—it was an act of surrender, a declaration that I believed He could use any tool, even a prescription, to bring restoration to my mind and body.

God put doctors on the earth for a reason. He is the Healer, but He often works through the wisdom and care of people He's gifted for that very purpose.

I left that office with a name for what I'd been battling: bipolar depression. It wasn't just a diagnosis; it was a breakthrough. In my hands were two prescriptions: a mood stabilizer and an antidepressant. But more than the medication, I left with a renewed sense of hope.

From that day forward, I began weaving medication into the fabric of my recovery. I leaned on the tools I had already built: a balanced diet, regular exercise, and the support of my Celebrate Recovery sponsor and church family. This wasn't a quick fix, but it was the start of a journey toward stability and self-understanding.

When Grace Runs in the Family

When I began finding relief through the new medication that helped balance my mood and strengthen my sobriety, I couldn't help but share it with my dad. I told him how much better I felt—most notably, less irritable—and how my emotions had steadied.

During one of dad's visits with us, I offered to help him make an appointment with our Psychiatric Nurse Practitioner, Mr. Kimuyu. My dad agreed to the appointment and invited me to sit in on the session. It felt sacred somehow—like I was witnessing God's hand bridging years of brokenness. Not long after they began to converse, Mr. Kimuyu smiled and said, "Angela, you didn't tell me your father was an Englishman." My dad chuckled.

It was an honor to sit beside him as he spoke about drinking every day and wanting to stop. Mr. Kimuyu listened intently, asking gentle questions that carried respect instead of shame. Before the appointment ended, he prescribed a medication that could help curb my dad's cravings for alcohol.

Just before his 70th birthday, around Thanksgiving of 2023, my dad stopped drinking. It felt like a divine reversal—the kind only God could orchestrate. The timing was no coincidence; it was as if Heaven itself was marking a generational turning point, sealing what God had begun in our family years earlier.

What I learned is that healing doesn't always come wrapped in worship songs and altar calls. Sometimes it shows up in doctors and therapy rooms. And maybe that's where redemption starts, when we stop waiting for perfect conditions to heal and say yes to the invitation God places in front of us. Even in the mess. Even in the questions. Healing found me.

There will come a day when I'll be able to wean off the medication completely — not through striving, but through wholeness. I trust God's perfect timing for that day. Until then, I live in gratitude for the tools He's provided and the peace that anchors my soul. Freedom, I've come to realize, isn't about being unassisted; it's about being unafraid to heal—body, soul, and spirit.

Reflection

What parts of your pain have you tried to fix on your own,
only to realize you needed help?
Where is God inviting you to see healing as holy,
even when it comes in unexpected forms?

The Lie Behind the Mask

"If I just pray harder, I won't need help.
If I'm strong enough, I won't need medicine."

The Truth

God uses both miracles and medicine.
Reaching for help isn't weakness—it's wisdom.

James 5:16 (NIV)
*Therefore confess your sins to each other and pray for each other so that you
may be healed. The prayer of a righteous person is powerful and effective.*

Scan to be led in a prayer of forgiveness and inner healing.

ACT IV

The Curtain Falls. Freedom Rises.

The final act reveals the unveiled bride—no longer hidden behind masks but standing fully known and fully loved. It's a season of forgiveness and radical freedom. Here, vulnerability becomes strength, prayer becomes a weapon, and intimacy is restored—both with God and others. This is the place where raw truth meets holy grace, and a new story of hope, love, and purpose unfolds.

CHAPTER TWENTY-FOUR

UNMASKED MARRIAGE

"To be loved but not known is comforting but superficial. To be known and not loved is our greatest fear. But to be fully known and truly loved is a lot like being loved by God."
—Timothy Keller

I came into my second marriage so broken, fighting battles I hadn't even named. When I married David, I had no idea that God was blessing me with far more than I imagined. He was inviting me to oneness, not just in covenant, but in vulnerability and healing.

This chapter isn't about a perfect marriage. It's about a perfect God who used a faithful man to gently uncover my guarded heart and show me the kind of love that stays and never let's go.

Love Without a Script

Shortly after we met, I invited David over to fix my children's bikes. I hadn't really cleaned the downstairs of my townhome in weeks, so I scrambled to declutter before he arrived. It was too hot to work outside, so we brought the bikes into the kitchen where he got to work. He repaired them without complaint and frustration. His calm demeanor caught me off guard.

A few days later, he stopped by after his daughter's softball game. As he stood near me in the living room, I felt a presence I had never experienced before. There was a peace about him that quieted my anxious spirit.

There were a few nights we didn't resist his staying over, and it was honestly bizarre to sleep next to a man who didn't try anything. Part of me expected him to make a move, just so I could relish the shock of saying no.

But his gentleness undid me the most. Riding in his truck felt foreign. He didn't yell at other drivers or weave in and out of traffic. My body, trained for chaos, didn't know how to relax in that kind of peace.

The real test came after we got married, when my kids carved tic-tac-toe into the hood of his red Toyota Tacoma with a coin. I braced for an explosion. But though he was understandably upset, he didn't rage. I had never seen a man with that kind of restraint.

As with most second and third marriages, the honeymoon phase didn't last long. Caring for my three young children left us exhausted. There were even times I accidentally called David by my first husband's name—a wound for both of us.

Being his third wife and having been Aaron's third wife before, fed a constant whisper: You're nobody's first choice. That lie played like a broken record, whispering that I was disposable, unworthy, too damaged to be loved. David had an uphill battle to prove otherwise.

Sometimes his attentiveness even irritated me. His hovering presence in the kitchen, what I used to call "clingy", felt intrusive.

He'd peel a banana before handing it to me. Unwrap my ice cream bar. These tiny gestures of care felt foreign, exposing just how unfamiliar I was with kindness. I had no reference for a man like him.

Before we married, I pretended I was into things I thought men wanted, like bringing another woman into our bedroom. Only to find David repulsed. His reaction shocked me and quietly restored a part of me I didn't know needed healing.

I tested him. Over and over. Pushing buttons, waiting for him to leave like everyone else had. My heart was fortified with walls. I needed to know if he could be trusted not to leave when things got hard.

Blending families didn't make things easier. Although David had daughters from a previous marriage, he had never dated women with kids, and now he had three stepchildren under his roof. One of our earliest hurdles was learning how to blend two families without letting our children divide us. We had to choose marriage first, or everything would crumble.

Blending a family is best done "low and slow," like a Texas brisket. We had to release control of what it "should" look like and commit to putting each other first, even when it felt selfish. For me, this was non-negotiable. I needed to know I was his first choice. Not second to anyone, not even to our children. David needed that from me too, especially while pieces of my heart still grieved Aaron.

I went from being divorced in January to remarried in July. There was no time to process, no time to heal. I pushed my children to call David, "Daddy David." It was my attempt at fixing the broken picture, but the quick transitions only made things harder.

David is meek, but he is not weak. He has an incredible tolerance for being mistreated but over time, even he began to voice his frustration.

While I was buried in my work, he became the steady one at home—faithful, reliable, and always present. His quiet nature made it easy for me to run from the chaos at home into the arms of a career. But he didn't want to be just the caretaker or the "house manager."

To quote again what my counselor once told me, "A halfway-healed person will attract a halfway-healed person." Our marriage was proof. We weren't just in love; we were codependent, each of us compensating for the other's brokenness.

Our meeting was divine intervention. I had been planning to move back to Michigan. David was praying for a wife chosen by God. But even as Spirit-filled believers, we carry scars. We weren't fighting each other—we were fighting the ghosts of our pasts. And quitting often felt easier than staying.

It took years before I truly believed David wouldn't leave me. I was convinced that one day he'd see me for who I was and walk away, just like the rest. That fear bled into every part of our relationship, even our sex life. Intimacy was hard. Without alcohol or marijuana, I didn't know how to let my guard down. I could give my body, but I didn't know how to give my heart.

God's idea of covenant marriage felt like a fairytale. I wasn't pure. I wasn't whole. I had worn the mask, but never the veil. I didn't feel like a bride. I felt like a harlot.

David had his own wounds—rejection, passivity, guilt. But somehow, our broken pieces fit together. We weren't perfect. We were just committed. And God began to build something holy in the cracks.

Becoming Team Martin

Once we had our child together, divorce became harder to imagine. It wasn't just about us anymore. I also knew how difficult it would be to raise my older son without David's steady presence. I leaned on him more than I wanted to admit.

But there was a season early on when I silently counted down the years until my son's graduation. I made a deal with myself. Just hang on, go through the motions, and leave when the time comes. It felt like mere survival. You can't have intimacy or a thriving marriage when your heart is halfway out the door.

I wore the Mask of Endurance, doing what I had to do to make it through. But my heart was hardened. I was missing the blessing God wanted to give me. But God had other plans.

Regardless of my intention or desire to leave, I still believed this marriage was better than the alternative of singleness and raising my children alone. But I had settled. I wasn't believing for more.

Eventually, we hit a breaking point. We were miserable. But we had invested too much to walk away without a fight. That's when we made a decision to become "Team Martin."

I saw it so clearly—a vision of David and I wearing matching football jerseys with Martin on the back. Every time I started to spiral into that familiar narrative, "Life would be so much better without him," I'd see that picture again. We were on the same team. We just needed to learn how to play together.

The Gift I Resisted

Physical touch was hard for me. Even simple gestures—hugging, kissing and even holding hands—felt intrusive. I assumed David was overly sensitive, but to him, my pulling away felt like rejection.

I didn't know how to be held without an agenda. Every touch, in my mind, felt like a setup to being used. I couldn't separate affection from manipulation because they had always been tangled together.

God used David to heal places in my heart I didn't even know were broken, but I fought Him every step of the way. I resisted the very thing God was using to restore me.

Healing, like heart surgery, never feels good at the time. It comes through friction and discomfort, through having your own walls mirrored back at you. David was my mirror. Grace became the glue that kept us together.

We were desperate for change and began seeking help on purpose. We attended marriage retreats, conferences, small groups, basically anything. Those spaces saved us. They gave us hope when we didn't have any left.

Over time, I learned what it meant to honor and respect David. I learned to trust him with my heart, something I had never done, not fully.

We agreed to stop using the "D" word. Divorce would no longer be an option. Just removing that word from our vocabulary changed everything. That gave us the correct language and tools to move forward.

The idea of real intimacy terrified me. Not just physical closeness, but soul-deep connection. I had spent years trying to fill a void with casual encounters that left me emptier each time. Sex without covenant had conditioned me to detach, and to believe that I wasn't worthy of lasting love. I didn't realize it then, but with every partner, I was eroding my ability to truly bond. So, when I finally had a relationship that was different, I dragged all that shame and regret with me.

I feared rejection. I wondered, "Am I enough? Will he compare me to someone else?" Betrayal, or your own soul feeling fractured from the past, makes it easy for intimacy to feel threatening.

As trust grew, we began to notice when our walls came down, and we stopped pretending. We started calling these moments, "taking off the fig leaves." It was our way of naming when we stopped hiding and started showing up as our true selves.

I remember the first time I felt naked and unashamed. I heard the Spirit whisper, "And the two shall become one."

We had been one flesh for years, but this was different. A spiritual union, not just a legal one. A design we heard about but didn't know how to live.

Sexual Healing

I knew I was carrying deep wounds when it came to sexual intimacy. You can't walk through a life of promiscuity, sin, and abuse without it leaving a mark. Some of the damage came from my own choices. Some of it came from things done to me that I didn't cause, didn't choose, and didn't deserve. Either way, the damage ran deep.

For a long time, I avoided sober sex. Being fully present meant being fully exposed, and I wasn't ready for that kind of vulnerability. I didn't know how, not even with someone I loved and trusted.

What I didn't expect was how God would bring healing through the very place I'd been most wounded. I know this might feel raw to read, but I'm going there for your sake. It would be unfair to talk about the sexual trauma from my past and not give the healing its due justice. Deep healing is possible when we surrender everything and stop holding back the parts of us that feel too broken and too painful. Trust Holy Spirit to lead you gently by the hand.

I broke soul ties with every past partner, including the ones I could barely remember. But sometimes, even in the most intimate moments with my David, memories would come flooding in and I'd feel a deep pain and anguish.

Sometimes I was more successful in hiding it. I wanted him to think I was enjoying him, but I was torn and distracted by the war deep within. He would be looking for my satisfaction, and I'd be weeping and eventually fall into his sweet embrace. It's hard to be intimate and receive pleasure from something that was a source of so much pain.

There were moments in our physical union when something deep inside me would break loose. It was the healing presence of God meeting us in our oneness. David was less concerned about having a release and began loving me in a way that made space for restoration. In becoming one flesh, I wasn't just experiencing physical intimacy. I was being made whole.

I also experienced moments outside of the bedroom that felt like spiritual heart surgery. The Lord would meet me in prayer, in worship, and begin to gently unravel the knots inside of me. What He was healing in my spirit began to spill over into my body, into my marriage. The more I let Him into those hidden places, the more I could trust David with the same.

True intimacy is risky. It's about being fully known and not fear being rejected. The Bible doesn't say Adam "had sex" with Eve. It says he knew her. That kind of knowing goes beyond physical touch. It's soul deep.

The Honeymoon of the Spirit

One of the hardest, and most holy shifts in our marriage came when we began to pray together. It didn't happen overnight, and it didn't come naturally, especially for David. I used to think we were the only ones fumbling through it, but when we started opening up with other couples in small groups, we realized we weren't alone.

Even though we both had our own personal prayer lives, there was this invisible wall when it came to praying together. That's because real prayer, especially as a couple, requires real vulnerability. And it's hard to pray when unforgiveness, bitterness, or hurts are in the way.

In the beginning, our prayers were short and awkward. We weren't just asking God to fix what was broken. We were asking Him to form something new in us.

There were times I didn't want to pray, especially when I was still hurting. But then I'd hear David's voice asking God for help and it would break through my defenses. His willingness to invite God into the conversation, even when I wasn't fully ready, began to soften my heart. Little by little, praying together became less awkward. We began to let down our defenses and simply made room for Him.

That's when we started to see how the enemy had subtly worked to keep us from praying in unity, because he knew the power that would be released when we did. And that power amplified into our sexual union. Prayer in that space became a weapon of warfare. What once divided us became the very place where we were made one.

The real honeymoon didn't happen at the beginning. It started to take shape about a decade into our marriage. Ironically, around the same time, many first marriages begin having to work harder to stay "in love." By then, I had four years of sobriety behind me, and our two middle kids had made it through the roughest stretch of adolescence.

Our foundation had been rebuilt, no longer fragile, but fortified. And just in time. What followed was a season of devastating loss, grief, relapse, a global pandemic, and a crisis with our youngest daughter. But this time, we stood side by side, united as one.

More Than a Fairytale

God has used our marriage in ways I never imagined. He has healed me, healed David, healed us. And in doing so, He has begun to heal our family, rewriting our story, and breaking the cycle of divorce that haunted us.

Whether you're married or longing to be, there is a covenant of marriage beyond your wildest imagination. Becoming the best version of yourself is the greatest gift you could give to your spouse and children.

As you have read all the personal struggles I had to overcome and heal from, I hope you realize that it is possible to rise from the ashes. You could rise as a precious bride, undefiled and redeemed.

Refuse to believe the lie that you're not valuable or worthy of real love. I now know that what once looked like a fairytale to me is achievable and even more so, fairytales don't compare to what God actually has made available to us. Thoughts such as "Every couple has infidelity, just to accept the inevitable" are a lie! God blessed my children and me with a man after God's own heart. And He can do the same for you.

God is still writing love stories. Yours may not look like mine, but I promise you this: when you invite Him into your healing, into your waiting, and into your union, He is faithful. He will redeem, restore, and rebuild what the enemy tried to destroy. There is still a kind of love that reflects the heart of God, waiting to be discovered.

What began as two broken stories has become a single unveiled song—a love that reflects the Bridegroom's heart, fierce and unending.

Through the slow unveiling of a love that doesn't quit, I've discovered the Bridegroom's heart for me. Every mask I tore away—self-reliance, shame, and fear—was met by a God who heals with both fire and tenderness. I stand here, not as a woman who has it all together, but as an unmasked and unveiled bride who is loved, chosen, and made whole.

Reflection

What walls have you built in marriage,
afraid that letting someone in will expose your wounds?
Where is God inviting you to trade survival for true unity?

The Lie Behind the Mask

"If I just endure, I'll be safe. If I stay guarded, I won't be hurt."

The Truth

True intimacy begins where self-protection ends. Love that lasts requires
vulnerability. God's design for marriage is not survival—it's oneness.

Ephesians 5:31 (NIV)
*For this reason a man will leave his father and mother and be united to
his wife, and the two will become one flesh.*

CHAPTER TWENTY-FIVE

STANDING OVATION: A LEGACY RESTORED

"Sometimes, the bravest and most important thing you can do is just show up."

—Brené Brown

An unexpected moment of deliverance came in November 2023, just before my 50th birthday. David and I were invited to dinner by the manager of a Brazilian steakhouse—someone we knew from *The Landing*, the Celebrate Recovery program for students where we all served together. He was from Brazil and often hosted a group of Brazilian pastors who gathered at the restaurant on Friday nights for dinner and prayer.

We had already eaten pizza at home, thinking we were only there to meet for the prayer gathering. But from the moment we arrived, we were treated like royalty—plates of perfectly seasoned meats, an endless salad bar, and even cheesecake set ablaze for dessert. After we were full beyond comfort, our host invited us into a private room where the ministers were finishing their meal and conversation.

We were warmly greeted by a couple—she was bilingual; he was not. Our friend translated as best he could while another pastor from Mexico, who spoke only Spanish, joined in. The discussion that followed, about Moses, Abraham, business, and ministry somehow reflected David's own journey. The restaurant had long since closed, but the Spirit was not finished.

As we stood to leave, the woman turned to David and began to prophesy. She spoke with authority about his calling, his leadership, and his role as a general in the faith. She encouraged him to rest, reminding him that even generals need rest. When David mentioned that he rarely slept more than four hours a night, they prayed for his sleep to be restored.

Then she turned toward me. I stood there, purse slung over my shoulder, quietly rejoicing over what had just been spoken about our business and family. But suddenly the atmosphere shifted. She began to speak to me about my need for rest and the spiritual attacks I'd been under. Her tone changed. She came closer, rebuking the spirit of fear and taking authority over every unclean spirit that had tried to invade our home.

The prayer intensified into full deliverance. Multiple ministers surrounded me, praying in tongues and declaring freedom over my life. Someone gently lifted the purse from my shoulder and guided me to sit in a chair as the power of God swept over me. Our friend called for another pastor who had already gone to his car; moments later, I heard his voice joining in, shouting with authority, "¡En el nombre de Jesús!"

I couldn't recall all the words, but I could feel the battle being won in the spirit. David stood nearby, and later filled in details I could barely remember. When the prayer lifted, the woman's tone softened. She looked at us with compassion and said, "The Lord is protecting your children. You are good parents. God is proud of you."

The room was filled with worship and praise as we sang out loud. We finally left the restaurant just after 1 a.m. My heart was light and overflowing. I felt like I was floating.

What's remarkable is that, before that night, I had been struggling with feeling down and empty of joy. But once again, the Holy Spirit set up a divine appointment for deliverance at a restaurant table.

It happened just weeks before I turned 50—the *Year of Jubilee*. In Scripture, Jubilee is the year when captives go free, debts are canceled, and land is restored. That night, I realized God was inviting me into my own Jubilee season—a time of freedom, rest, and restoration. The spirit of fear had lost its grip. I was stepping into a new decade unmasked and fully at rest in His love.

A New Legacy Begins

While my children were growing up, I used to tell them, "If you can survive me being your mom, then you can survive anything in life." I wasn't trying to be funny. It was a hard truth. I was barely present during the chaos of my first marriage, the heartbreak of divorce, the struggles of single parenting three children, and remarrying before either of us had healed.

Add to that a long-term drug addiction and an undiagnosed mental illness, and it was a lot for anyone to survive. Then came the devastating death of their father, which shook us all to the core. But now, those years are being restored.

Despite our history, my children aren't in a horrible place. They've been raised in a safe environment with growing stability. Since 2014, I've been working on my recovery, and they've had a front-row seat to my transformation. They've watched me live unfiltered, not hiding the truth or pretending everything was fine. I've walked this out in front of them with honesty and humility.

I live for legacy, not for applause. I parent my adult children and grandchildren from a place of wisdom, compassion, and a sound mind. I'm pointing them toward the path I found.

Where the Spirit Met the Shore

On August 1, 2025, our friend Daniel invited David on a chartered fishing trip off the coast of Freeport, Texas. Before long, the invitation expanded to include me and our two sons, Andrew and Aaron. I was thrilled, not only for the blessing of the trip itself but for the rare opportunity to spend time together as a family. Aaron, 24, had just moved out at the end of May, and we hadn't had much time with him since.

The trip turned out to be a wonderful experience for all of us—reeling in red snappers and kingfish. I even caught the largest kingfish of the day! The next morning, before heading home, we spent time in the ocean while the boys fished from the shore.

At some point that day, Aaron and I began talking about God and healing from our past hurts. Daniel joined in, sharing parts of his own life and recovery journey. Then, in what felt like a divinely orchestrated moment, the Holy Spirit met us there on the beach.

Aaron opened up and told me how, in the past, he had sought relationships with women to fill a void and a deep longing to be nurtured, but in ways that were unhealthy. As he spoke, I felt prompted to act on a gentle thought: *Give him a long hug—one that lasts long enough to release healing.*

I wrapped my arms around him, and he didn't pull away. In fact, he leaned in, fully embracing the moment. I looked at him, asked him to take off his sunglasses, and said softly, "I'm sorry for not nurturing you the way you needed me to. But it's not too late to start now."

The presence of God surrounded us there by the water. We hugged again and again. Tears streamed down my face as I began to prophesy over him. It was a holy, healing moment.

Since that day, things have been different. Most mornings now begin with a text from Aaron telling me he loves me and wishing me a blessed day. God is truly restoring the years the enemy tried to steal.

A Hug that Healed Generations

On August 9, 2025, the weekend before David's 60th birthday, I pulled off a surprise party for him at a local country-western dance hall, surrounded by friends and family. My sister, Sheila, even made a six-hour trip to celebrate with us. I hadn't seen or spoken with her much since my own 50th birthday, nearly two years earlier; so her being there already felt like a gift from God.

The next day, Sheila called to say that Andrew had invited her over and jokingly asked if it was okay to stop by. She had some time before dinner plans with her daughter, so I told her to come. When she arrived, she came into our home relaxed and comfortable. For the first time in years, I didn't feel the old barriers between us.

We sat together on the couch, talking about our parents, their quirks, and the patterns we had begun to notice in their relationship. To my surprise, we found ourselves in agreement, not opposition. Then the conversation turned to something simple—she mentioned a knee injury from walking one of her dogs. I related, telling her that my own knee had been bothering me lately too, though I wasn't sure why.

Then came a gentle prompting in my spirit: *"Pray for one another."*

I invited David to join us, and the three of us prayed together. As we laid hands and prayed, I felt another nudge from the Holy Spirit—to offer Sheila one of those long hugs that lasts more than 20 seconds. As we stood there embracing, the presence of God filled the room. Without hesitation, I began to take authority over the old spirit of jealousy that had shadowed our family line for generations. Words rose up from deep within me—I rebuked the spirit, broke the generational curse spoken over us as children, and began to shout and rejoice that it was finished in Jesus' name!

Sheila looked at me, eyes brimming with tears. "Wait," she said softly.

"This is important. There's something I need to tell you." She paused.

"At home, in my bathroom, I have a picture of us when we were about three and four. I keep it there to remind me to pray for you—because of all the people I've had to forgive, you've been the hardest." Her words pierced my heart, but not with pain. This time, it was release. The power of God was thick in the air. The very spirit that had divided us since childhood was being uprooted before our eyes. What an amazing and powerful God we serve!

Later, when I shared the story with my mom over the phone, she immediately began praying in the Spirit, her voice rising with power and authority. She began partnering in the moment of redemption—reclaiming our family line and praising God.

The fire of the Holy Spirit ignited in her so powerfully that even my dad, sitting in the next room, couldn't ignore it. Heaven had joined the conversation, and there was no quenching the move of the Spirit that day. It was a holy moment. A generational shift. The curse was broken, and what once divided us was now redeemed by love.

Generations are changing because I chose to stop the madness and break the cycle of dysfunction. It takes laying down pride. It takes stillness. It takes the courage to step off the hamster wheel long enough to look in the mirror and choose something different. Change is hard. If it weren't, more people would do it.

Hear this. The cycle ends with you! The darkness that tried to consume you is a backdrop to the radiant light you are. There is a fullness of life waiting for you, one where your scars tell a story of triumph, and your voice speaks freedom into existence for generations to come.

My life is living proof to my children that God is redeeming our bloodline, one generation at a time.

Reflection

The final bow isn't an ending—it's a revealing. God is restoring what was stripped away by shame, addiction, fear, or loss.
You no longer need the masks to survive; you can stand unveiled and unashamed, radiant in His redemption.
What if the years you thought were wasted were actually the soil of your becoming?

The Lie Behind the Mask

"It's too late for me to step into purpose or joy."

The Truth

God wastes nothing. Every season of pain, delay, and disappointment becomes a seed of restoration in His hands. What felt stolen will be returned in multiplied form—beauty for ashes, glory for shame, and purpose for every tear. You are being unveiled.

Joel 2:25 (NIV)

God's promise to you and me, *"I will restore to you the years that the swarming locust has eaten, the hopper, the destroyer, and the cutter, my great army, which I sent among you."*

Romans 8:28 (NKJV)

And we know that all things work together for good to those who love God, to those who are the called according to His purpose.

EPILOGUE

The curtain has fallen. The script is no longer in my hands. I've walked off the stage, not in defeat but in divine freedom. There will be no encore, no more pretending, no more performing. This is the part of the story where I step fully into who I was created to be: unmasked and undeniably free.

You were never meant to perform your way into belonging. You were formed to carry the glory of God, not the expectations of others. The same God who met me in the depths of despair will meet you in your place of hiding. And He won't just pull you out. He'll walk you out, hand in hand, into the life you didn't dare dream was possible.

The stage was never your home. Freedom is.

The shattered pieces are the very material God uses to build legacy. Your story isn't over. It's just getting honest. And honesty is where the power begins.

This journey isn't about being cured. It's been about becoming whole. About trading shame for significance. About learning that healing isn't always tidy, but it is always holy. I didn't arrive at perfection. I arrived at presence. God's presence. And in that place, I discovered I could live on purpose, in purpose, for a purpose.

You don't need a platform to be powerful. You don't need a spotlight to shine. And you don't need applause to make an impact.

What you need is permission—and I'm giving it to you now. Permission to walk in progress instead of chasing perfection. Permission to take off the mask and find His hand waiting.

Look at yourself, not with judgment, but with grace. This is your moment to step forward, to embrace healing, to own your story without shame.

You don't have to do it all today. Just one step. Just one whispered "yes" to freedom, and the weight of shame, fear, and despair will begin lifting.

My life serves as a witness that Jesus still rewrites stories. And yours is next. No more pretending, no more acting. I declare a breakthrough over your life!

So, take a bow—not for performance, but for surviving.

Take a breath—not to prepare for another act, but to inhale the truth.

And then, rise and take your place.

Not on stage, but in the center of God's plan for your life. Because the bravest thing you can do? Walk off the stage... and live.

Today, I am exposed—not perfect, not cured, but free. And that freedom is worth every step of the journey.

Scan to step fully into freedom and live unmasked.

THE VISION OF THE RADIANT BRIDE

Designing the cover for *Unmasked* was one of the most challenging—and sacred—parts of this journey. From the beginning, I knew I wanted an image that reflected the theme of unmasking, so my designer and I explored a masquerade concept. The first two designs were beautiful, but something in my spirit felt unsettled. They looked right, yet they didn't *feel* right.

While visiting my parents one weekend, I reviewed the mockups again. The next morning, I awoke with a line from William Shakespeare's *As You Like It* echoing in my mind: *"All the world's a stage, and all the men and women merely players."* Instantly, it resonated. My story is a stage play—a journey of performing different roles, wearing different masks, and finally stepping into authenticity.

A few days later, as I prayed in my writing room, I received a vision: roses being thrown onto a stage at the end of a performance. Then I saw myself walking off that stage—my mask left behind, my script torn, no longer performing. The scene ended with me unveiled and unashamed, standing radiant as a bride. That's when I knew: *this* was the cover.

To honor that vision, I chose to wear my mother's wedding dress—a symbol of legacy, restoration, and generational healing. I'm deeply grateful to the creative souls who helped bring this vision to life. It took time (and a bit of my perfectionist nature!), but what you now hold in your hands is the truest reflection of my story.

RESOURCES

As you step into freedom and begin unmasking your own story, these resources can guide you toward support, wisdom, and healing. Every resource listed here has been trusted by others on similar journeys of recovery and spiritual growth.

Hotlines

- **National Suicide Prevention Lifeline**
  Free, confidential support for anyone in crisis.
  1-800-273-TALK (8255)

- **Crisis Text Line**
  Immediate emotional support via text.
  Text HOME to 741741

- **Human Trafficking Hotline**
  Support and resources for victims of human trafficking.
  1-888-373-7888

- **Domestic Abuse Hotline**
  Assistance and guidance for domestic violence situations.
  1-800-799-7233

Books

- **The Holy Bible**
  The foundational text of the Christian faith, offering guidance, wisdom, and the promise of salvation.

- **Emotionally Healthy Spirituality – Peter Scazzero**
  Learn how to integrate emotional health with your spiritual life and grow in both.

- **Life's Healing Choices – John Baker**
  Practical guidance for breaking free from unhealthy patterns and choosing God's path for healing.

- **Boundaries – Dr. Henry Cloud**
  Insights on setting healthy limits and protecting emotional, mental, and spiritual well-being.

- **Jesus Calling – Sarah Young**
  Daily devotional insights to encourage intimacy with God and trust in His guidance.

- **The Secret Power of Speaking God's Word – Joyce Meyer**
  A guide to applying the power of God's Word in everyday life for transformation and victory.

Support Groups

- **Celebrate Recovery | celebraterecovery.com**
  Christ-centered recovery program for anyone struggling with hurts, habits, or hang-ups.

- **Divorce Care | divorcecare.org**
  Support for those recovering from divorce or separation.

- **Grief Share | griefshare.org**
  Support groups for navigating the loss of a loved one.

Mental Health Resources

- **Depression and Bipolar Support Alliance | dbsalliance.org**
  Support and resources for individuals with mood disorders and trauma.

- **SAMHSA – Substance Abuse and Mental Health Services Administration | samhsa.org**
  Information and recovery support for mental health and substance use disorders.

Counseling

- **Above and Beyond Christian Counseling | aandbcounseling.com**
  Faith-based counseling to support emotional and spiritual health.

Physical Health

- **Integrative Primary Care | livewell-medsolutions.com**
  Integrative medical solutions for overall wellness.

- **Bill Dasch Ministries | billdasch.com**
  Healing prayer and resources for emotional, physical, and spiritual restoration.

Financial Health

- **Ramsey Solutions | ramseysolutions.com**
  Resources and coaching for personal financial growth and stewardship.

Marriage & Family

- **XO Marriage | xomarriage.com**
  Practical tools to strengthen and restore marriages.

- **Family Life | familylife.com**
  Biblical guidance for marriage, parenting, and family relationships.

- **Focus on the Family | focusonthefamily.com**
  Support and resources for marriage and family challenges.

- **As For Me & My House Ministries | rondeal.org**
  Guidance and coaching for navigating blended family life.

ACKNOWLEDGEMENTS

To my beloved husband, **David**—you have loved me beyond anything I could have ever imagined. Your steadfast faith in God and your intercessory prayers have fueled my healing, deliverance, and every success along the way. As I've told you many times, there's no way I could make it without you. Our family stands fortified because of your unwavering faith, love, and protection. You have been my anchor through every storm and my safe place in every season. Words will never be enough to express the depth of my gratitude for you. I will spend the rest of our lives showing you just how much I adore you and the beautiful life we've built together. You are, and will always be, the love of my life.

To my incredible parents—**Mom and Dad**—I honor you and love you both deeply. I thank God that He chose you to be my parents. The seeds you've planted in me are now bearing much fruit. Your generous hearts have loved me through the most painful seasons of my life, and never once did I doubt your love. We are now living in the restoration you both fought for—through your faith, perseverance, and love for God. Your legacy is seen, felt, and will echo for generations to come.

To my siblings—**Sheila, Tonia, and Trevor**—I am so blessed to have each of you in my life and thank God for the healing and restoration in our relationships. I love you all dearly and am grateful for the bond we share.

To my sponsor and friend, **Heather Craig**—you have walked beside me through a decade of healing and recovery. Your steadfast example and authentic life have continually challenged me to grow, to heal, and to rise higher. I could never thank you enough for your prayers, your wisdom, and your unwavering support. My success—and the legacy that flows from it—is yours to share.

To my writing coach, **Colette Toach**—you have challenged me, stretched me, and guided me from writer to author. This book is as much yours as mine. Thank you for believing in me and for mining the gold that was hidden within. Through your mentorship, I've grown not only in skill but in confidence, clarity, and calling. Your investment has shaped both my message and my ministry, and I am forever grateful.

To my recovery sisters—**Angela, Shauna, Michele, and Heather**—you have all helped me more than you know. There were times when you sought my guidance, and I was barely holding on myself. Walking alongside each of you in your struggles has released even more grace and power into my life, teaching me to surrender again and again. Thank you for trusting me to impart grace and strength to you; our journey together has been a gift beyond measure.

To my pastors and dear friends, **Steve and Jeana Pixler**—your teaching has transformed my mind, and your care has propelled me into this *kairos* moment. Thank you for believing in me and giving me the space to grow in both leadership and ministry. Your example of humility, wisdom, and Spirit-led vision continues to inspire me. I joyfully follow you as you follow Christ.

To my **Freedom Life Church** and **Friday Night Prayer family**, who have stood by me, encouraged me, prayed me through, and continued to hold up my arms—your love for me is felt. When I wanted to quit and hide away, *you* reminded me of who I was and helped me keep going.

Your faithfulness has been a lifeline, and your love a reflection of God's own heart. My heart is full because of you.

Thank you to all who invested financially in this project. Your support held me accountable to keep writing when I wanted to quit. May the seeds you planted bear eternal fruit, and may your investment be richly rewarded in ways only God can reveal.

To my editor, **Melissa Chavez**—I am so blessed that God allowed our paths to cross. You have been an answer to prayer. Thank you for your excellence, your diligence, and the anointing you carry—it rests upon these pages. Your touch has brought clarity, beauty, and flow to this message, and I am deeply grateful.

ABOUT THE AUTHOR

Angela L. Martin is a passionate entrepreneur, ministry leader, and recovery mentor. She co-owns **DM Roofing TX** with her husband and partners in **Uplift Elevator, LLC**, blending business excellence with a heart for serving others. A devoted wife and mother, Angela cherishes family as the foundation of her life and ministry. Through *Get Real With Angela*, she mentors those navigating addiction, shame, and grief, guiding them toward healing and hope. As **Prayer Team Leader** at **Freedom Life Church**, she intercedes for her community and empowers others to step into spiritual authority. Angela and her husband David build their businesses and ministry by faith, leaving a legacy of transformation and lasting impact for generations.